Man From Tennessee

Johnnie Day

ISBN: Number

Published by:

Columbus Book Publishers

www.columbusbookpublishers.com

Printed in the United States of America

Dedication

For my sister, Martha, whose unwavering strength and resilience inspired this story. This book is a testament to the enduring bonds of family, the courage it takes to face adversity, and the unyielding hope that can carry us through even the darkest of times. It's a dedication to the unsung heroes, the quiet souls who persevere in the face of hardship, often unnoticed, their contributions overlooked in the grand narrative of history. This narrative aims to illuminate their strength and their stories, a small tribute to the countless individuals who migrated westward, seeking a new life, facing danger and uncertainty with a quiet dignity that deserves to be remembered.

This dedication is also for those who journeyed across the vast and unforgiving landscapes of the American frontier, who braved the elements, the hostility of both man and nature, the isolation and uncertainty that tested their spirits. They were the pioneers, the trailblazers, the unsung heroes whose contributions shaped the destiny of a nation. They weren't always the bold, larger-than-life figures often depicted in romanticized narratives; they were ordinary individuals grappling with extraordinary challenges. They faced loss, hardship, and disappointment, yet they endured, driven by a profound sense of hope and determination.

This story, with all its trials and tribulations, is an attempt to capture their essence, honor their spirit, and commemorate their often-forgotten sacrifices. They faced prejudice, injustice, and violence, yet they clung to their dreams, their families, and their hopes for a better future. May this dedication serve as a small token of appreciation for their unwavering courage, their unshakeable spirit, and their indelible contribution to the history of this nation. May their stories resonate through the pages and linger in the hearts of those who have read their epic and often overlooked struggles.

Their legacies are not etched in stone or monuments but are woven into the very fabric of the American spirit, a constant reminder of the human capacity for endurance and resilience in the face of overwhelming odds. This is their story, in essence, and it is told with respect, admiration, and gratitude for their quiet bravery and strength. For women and men alike who faced the unknown with courage and grace, this book is dedicated to their memory and to the powerful legacy they left behind.

Acknowledgment

My deepest gratitude goes to my wife, Susan, whose unwavering support and patience made this book possible. Her insightful critiques and tireless editing were invaluable. Thanks also to my editor, Johnathan Blake, for his guidance and belief in this story. I am indebted to the numerous historians and researchers whose work provided the backdrop for this novel. Special thanks to Professor Emily Carter of the University of Wyoming for her assistance with historical details concerning the settlement of Dust Devil Gulch and the economic challenges faced by early pioneers in the region. Finally, I thank the countless individuals who shared their stories and insights, enriching my understanding of the spirit of the American West.

About the Author

Johnnie Day, residing in Rockwood Tennessee is a Western novelist and historian whose passion for the American West is reflected in his meticulous research and evocative storytelling. He spent years immersed in the history of Wyoming, visiting historical sites, studying archival materials, and interviewing descendants of early pioneers. Johnnie's previous works include [list of previous books] and his novels have been praised for their accurate portrayal of the period, their compelling characters, and their thrilling narratives. He currently resides in [location].

Table of Contents

Chapter 1 Leaving Home Behind... 1

Chapter 2 A Perilous Journey Begins.................................... 7

Chapter 3 First Encounters on the Trail........................... 14

Chapter 4 Navigating Unfamiliar Territory..................... 20

Chapter 5 A Chance Encounter 26

Chapter 6 The Vastness of Wyoming................................ 33

Chapter 7 Tribal Encounters... 39

Chapter 8 Survival on the Plains 47

Chapter 9 A Desperate Alliance 53

Chapter 10 The Pursuit Begins 60

Chapter 11 Entering the Mountains.................................. 66

Chapter 12 Mountain Ambush 72

Chapter 13 A Narrow Escape... 78

Chapter 14 Betrayal and Trust.. 83

Chapter 15 A Glimmer of Hope... 89

Chapter 16 Reunion and Relief... 95

Chapter 17 Unraveling the Mystery.. 102

Chapter 18 Facing the Conspiracy... 108

Chapter 19 Unexpected Allies 114

Chapter 20 Preparing for Confrontation... 120

Chapter 21 The Final Confrontation 125

Chapter 22 A Desperate Fight for Survival..................................... 131

Chapter 23 Justice Prevails.. 137

Chapter 24 Unexpected Losses 143

Chapter 25 A Moment of Reflection 149

Chapter 26 Life after the Storm 155

Chapter 27 A New Normal.. 162

Chapter 28 Looking Toward the Future.. 168

Chapter 29 The Legacy of the West.................................... 173

Epilogue A New Dawn 179

Glossary.. 185

Chapter 1
Leaving Home Behind

The air hung heavy with the scent of woodsmoke and damp earth, a familiar perfume that Elias Thorne, a man etched by the sun and weathered by time, inhaled deeply one last time. His late thirties bore the weight of years spent tilling the rich Tennessee soil, a life now abruptly severed by a telegram—a desperate plea from his sister, Sarah, stranded in the unforgiving wilderness of Wyoming Territory. The ink on the telegram had been hurried, the handwriting shaken—fear lived in those words. He stood on the porch of his modest farmhouse, the setting sun casting long shadows that stretched and distorted the familiar landscape, mirroring the unease in his heart. The worn clapboard of the house, the weathered fence posts, and the familiar sway of the nearby oaks—all were soon to become memories.

His gaze lingered on the rolling hills that dipped and swooped in the fading light, a landscape he knew intimately, each curve and rise etched in his memory as surely as the lines on his face. Tonight, however, those hills were nothing but the ghosts of a past he was about to leave behind. Little did he know that this might be his last sunset here. The farm, his sanctuary, his legacy—it held the echoes of a life lived modestly, a life he was now leaving behind. A life filled with the comforting rhythm of seasons, the satisfaction of honest toil, and the quiet companionship of his neighbors, faces that would now blur into the tapestry of memories.

He ran a calloused hand over the worn wooden frame of a photograph clutched in his other hand. It depicted a younger Sarah, a radiant girl with bright eyes and a mischievous smile, a stark contrast to the gaunt and desperate woman described in the urgent telegram. The image was faded, almost sepia-toned with age. Yet, it held a vividness that transcended the discoloration, a potent reminder of the sister he was bound to protect, the reason for this agonizing farewell.

The decision to leave hadn't been easy. It was a wrenching separation from everything he knew, a leap into the unknown. He'd spent weeks debating, the pros and cons weighing heavily on his soul. The comfortable familiarity of his life in Tennessee was a powerful anchor, pulling him back from the treacherous currents of the unknown West.

Yet, the desperate plea in his sister's telegram, the underlying fear, and the vulnerability in her words ultimately shattered the comforting illusion of security. Family loyalty, a deep-rooted principle forged in the crucible of his upbringing, superseded every other consideration.

The simple act of packing was a painful process, each item chosen carefully, representing a facet of his life. A worn-out, leather-bound Bible, a testament to his faith; a few sturdy tools symbolizing his skill and self-reliance; a small bag of dried beans and cornmeal, a meager sustenance for the long and arduous journey ahead. Every object held a memory, a whisper of a past he was leaving behind, a past that now seemed distant and unreal, like a half-remembered dream.

As twilight deepened, the final vestiges of the day faded into the embrace of darkness. Neighbors, their faces etched with concern and understanding, gathered at the edge of his property. There were no boisterous farewells, no grand pronouncements, just a quiet exchange of knowing glances and a solemn understanding. These were simple folk, their lives intertwined by the shared rhythms of rural existence, and their unspoken support was a balm to Elias's aching heart. There were handshakes, gruff words of encouragement, and the unspoken promise of a future reunion; a fragile hope clung against looming uncertainty.

Man From Tennessee

Old Man Fitzwilliam, his face a roadmap of wrinkles etched by time and toil, placed a weathered hand on Elias's shoulder. "Take care, son," he rasped, his voice hoarse from years of shouting over the wind. "The West ain't for the faint of heart. But you've got the grit, I reckon." His words, though simple, resonated deeply, reinforcing Elias's resolve. He had the grit and determination, but the sheer scale of the task that loomed before him, a daunting prospect that filled him with a mixture of trepidation and grim determination.

He couldn't sleep the night before he left. His gun rested against the railing as he sat on the porch, the rocking rocker groaning under his weight. There was a spooky silence, the kind that falls before a storm. Was he being lured into something he wouldn't come back from, or was the West his calling?

He spent the final moments in the stillness of the night, and the only sounds were the chirping of crickets and the rustling of leaves in the gentle night breeze. He sat on the porch swing, the worn wood creaking beneath his weight, gazing at the star-studded sky, a vast canvas of infinite possibilities and unknown dangers. The worn photograph of Sarah clutched in his hand, the image a beacon of hope under the swift encroaching darkness. The weight of his journey began to settle heavily on him, but the unshakeable resolve in his eyes betrayed no sign of wavering. He was leaving everything behind, yet he carried with him the indomitable spirit of a man bound by duty, driven by his unwavering love for his sister.

The following day dawned clear and crisp, the air sharp and invigorating, a stark contrast to the heavyweight in his heart. He hoisted his meager pack onto his weary shoulders, its weight a physical manifestation of his burdens.

He paused one last time, his eyes tracing the familiar contours of his farm, his home, a place he would likely never see again. The silence of the morning was broken only by the gentle creak of the gate as he passed through it, closing it behind him firmly. It was a final gesture, a decisive step into the uncertain future that lay ahead. He mounted his trusty steed, a steadfast companion in this perilous venture, and set off toward the West, the rising sun painting the sky in hues of hope and fear. The journey had begun.

With every mile stretching behind him, Tennessee blurred into a fading memory. Ahead, only uncertainty awaited.

The miles were long and the dangers many, but a fierce and unwavering determination burned in his heart. His sister's life depended on him in the vast, unforgiving expanse of the

Man From Tennessee

Wyoming Territory, a landscape as vast and unknown as the challenges he would soon face. He rode toward the setting sun, a silhouette against the rising dawn, a lone figure embarking on a journey that would test his mettle, his resolve, and the essence of his being. The journey was fraught with peril, but he would not waver. His sister needed him. And Elias Thorne, man of the Tennessee soil, was going to find her.

Chapter 2
A Perilous Journey Begins

The first few days were a blur of dust and sweat, the familiar comfort of Tennessee roads fading behind him like a receding dream. The rolling hills, once a source of solace, gradually gave way to expansive plains, stretching out before him like a sea of tallgrass. The change was mirrored within him, a slow, almost imperceptible shift from the rooted stability of his past life to the tentative, uncertain footing of his present journey. The air grew drier, the scent of woodsmoke replaced by the sharp, clean tang of prairie wind. His trusty steed, a powerful sorrel named Buck, plodded steadily onward, his rhythmic gait a steady counterpoint to the drumming of Elias's heart. With each passing day, as civilization began to emerge, roads turned to trails, trails then becoming mere impressions on earth. The world was about to get much wilder.

He encountered others on the trail, a motley crew of travelers heading west for various reasons. There was Jedediah, a grizzled prospector with eyes that held the glint of both hope and cynicism, his weathered face a testament to years spent chasing fool's gold under the merciless sun. Jedediah shared stories of lost fortunes and narrow escapes, his voice a gravelly whisper against the backdrop of the whispering wind. He spoke of hidden canyons and treacherous rivers, of the unforgiving nature of the land and the even more unforgiving nature of some of its inhabitants. His tales, while laced with dark humor that belied the harsh realities they depicted, served as a sobering reminder of the dangers ahead.

Then there was Martha, a young widow traveling with her two children, their faces pale and thin from the hardship of their journey. She was bound for Oregon, seeking a new life away from the grief and poverty that had become her constant companions.

Martha's hands trembled when she spoke of her late husband, the fear in her eyes unmistakable. "We keep moving," she whispered, "because stopping means being found."

Danger wasn't just whispered about—it lingered. Elias saw it in the skeletal remains of abandoned wagons and in the buzzards circling too close for comfort. Each night, as he built his fire, he would vigilantly listen to the sounds beyond the flickering lights.

A Perilous Journey Begins

Her quiet dignity in the face of adversity touched Elias
deeply, reminding him of the strength he would need to draw
upon in the coming months. They shared a quiet supper one
evening, the meager fare a testament to the shared experiences
that bound them together. He patiently listened as she spoke of
her late husband, of her hopes and fears for her children, her
voice filled with a quiet desperation that mirrored the
uncertainty of her future. He found himself sharing some of his
own burdens, his words finding unexpected solace in the
shared silence of the campfire. Their brief companionship was
a fleeting moment of human connection, a reminder that
human kindness could still flourish even in the vast emptiness
of the frontier.

The days melted into weeks, each sunrise heralding
another stretch of arduous miles. Elias learned to read the
subtle shifts in the landscape, anticipate the changing weather,
and judge the quality of water sources. His farming skills
proved invaluable, and his knowledge of plants and survival
techniques allowed him to supplement his meager supplies. He
discovered edible roots and berries and learned to track game
with growing expertise, his movements becoming increasingly
fluid and efficient as he adapted to the rhythms of the frontier.
He learned to be self-sufficient, relying on his resourcefulness

and his ability to adapt to constantly shifting circumstances. Each hardship encountered along the way strengthened his resolve, hardening him to the harsh realities of the journey.

He learned to trust his instincts, to read the signs of approaching danger. He often rode with his rifle across his lap, his hand never far from the trigger. He encountered hostile wildlife—a lone mountain lion that watched him from a rocky outcrop, its eyes gleaming like twin embers in the twilight, and a pack of wild dogs that circled his camp one night; their hungry snarls a chilling prelude to a potential attack. He handled such encounters with a calm efficiency honed by years of living close to nature; his years on the Tennessee farm, though far removed from the wilds of the Western frontier, had equipped him with unique skills that served him well.

The landscape continued to change, the endless plains gradually giving way to rugged canyons and towering mountains, their jagged peaks piercing the sky like the teeth of some ancient beast. The vastness of the landscape was both awe-inspiring and overwhelming, a constant reminder of the enormity of his undertaking. The journey tested his physical endurance, mental fortitude, and very spirit. But amidst the hardship, there was also a strange beauty, a wildness that captivated him, a testament to the raw power of the natural world.

He crossed rivers that swelled with spring runoff, their currents fierce and unpredictable, testing the strength of Buck and Elias's courage and skill. He navigated treacherous mountain passes, the air thin and biting, and the path narrow and precarious. He weathered sudden storms that seemed to rage from nowhere, their violence a shocking reminder of the unpredictable nature of the frontier. Each obstacle presented a new challenge, demanding both physical and mental resilience, testing his limits in ways he never thought possible.

While making camp near a rushing stream one evening, he stumbled upon a small band of Lakota Sioux. Their initial reaction was cautious, their eyes wary, evaluating him as a potential threat. Elias, remembering Jedediah's warnings about the tensions between settlers and Native Americans, approached them respectfully, offering them a small gift of tobacco. He spoke slowly and deliberately, avoiding sudden movements, and his demeanor was calm and non-threatening.

Through a series of gestures and a few broken words of their language, he communicated his peaceful intentions, explaining his reasons for traveling west.

Man From Tennessee

To his surprise, the Lakota proved to be wary yet not hostile. Their initial apprehension slowly gave way to curiosity, and Elias found himself welcomed into their camp and offered food and shelter for the night. He learned from them about the land, the hidden trails and water sources, the wisdom of the elders, and the respect for the natural world.

He shared stories of his life back east, offering a glimpse into a world far removed from their own. Their interaction provided a valuable lesson in cross-cultural understanding, highlighting the complexities of living on the frontier and the importance of diplomacy and respect.

The next morning, after a heartfelt farewell, Elias continued his journey, his heart filled with a profound sense of respect and admiration for the Lakota people. The encounter had not only refreshed his supplies but also strengthened his understanding of the diverse people inhabiting this vast and unforgiving land, reminding him that the journey was about overcoming physical challenges and navigating the delicate relationships between different cultures.

The journey was wearing him down, but his determination remained unshaken. His sister's image remained vivid in his mind, her face a beacon of hope against the backdrop of the vast and lonely landscape. He pressed onward, the rising sun

A Perilous Journey Begins

each morning a promise of progress, a testament to his unwavering resolve. The West was wild, unforgiving, and beautiful, and he was slowly but surely making his way across it. The perilous journey had begun, and Elias Thorne, a man of the Tennessee soil, was going to reach his destination, whatever the cost.

Chapter 3
First Encounters on the Trail

The sun dipped below the horizon, painting the sky in fiery orange and deep purple hues, a breathtaking spectacle that offered little comfort to Elias. He ought to have paused to appreciate it, but his stomach churned in discomfort. The long day's ride had left him weary, his muscles aching, his throat parched. He'd found a relatively sheltered spot near a rocky outcrop, intending to make camp and rest before the darkness fully descended. As he dismounted Buck, the sorrel whinnying softly, a prickling sensation ran down Elias's spine. It wasn't the usual creak of the settling earth or the rustle of nocturnal creatures in the tall grass; something else pulled his nerves to the edge.

The air, usually crisp and clean, felt heavy and thick with an almost palpable tension. He scanned the surrounding landscape, his eyes tracing the shadows cast by the dying light. He saw nothing initially, but the feeling persisted, a low hum of unease that vibrated in the silence. Then... he saw them.

Man From Tennessee

Three figures, silhouetted against the fading light, emerged from the shadows. They moved with a predatory grace, their movements fluid and silent, like ghosts in the gathering dusk. They were a distance away, but Elias's keen eyes, honed by years of living off the land, instantly recognized the telltale signs of outlaws: the slouch of their postures, the careless way they carried themselves, the glint of metal—likely knives or pistols—at their hips. The sight sent a cold wave of fear washing over him, a stark reminder of the dangers lurking beneath the seemingly tranquil surface of the frontier.

He assessed his situation rapidly, his mind working with the efficiency he had honed during years of navigating the unpredictable challenges of his farm life. His rifle, thankfully, was still within easy reach, resting across his saddle. Sensing the shift in Elias's demeanor, Buck snorted softly, his ears pricked up, his stance shifting from relaxed to alert. The outlaws were still some distance away, but they were closing in, their movements deliberate... their intent clear.

Elias's fingers itched for his rifle, but he knew better— pulling first might mean dying first. Elias knew he couldn't risk a confrontation. He was alone, outnumbered, and weary from his long journey. A direct fight would be foolhardy, suicidal even. His survival depended on his wits, stealth, and knowledge of the terrain. He made a silent prayer for his sister and slowly and deliberately began preparing to move.

He quickly gathered his few belongings—a small pouch of food, his water skin, and a blanket—securing them in his saddlebags. He checked the flint and steel for his fire, ensuring it was ready for immediate use. The entire process was performed with an almost unnatural calm, his heart hammering in his chest, but his movements were controlled and precise. Every fiber of his being screamed at him to flee, to run, but he knew that a panicked retreat could easily turn into a desperate chase, leaving him vulnerable and exposed. Elias made himself remain motionless. They would jump at the first hint of abrupt movement.

He needed a plan. He glanced around, studying the rocky outcrop, searching for an escape route. He spotted a narrow cleft in the rocks, barely visible in the diminishing light that could provide some cover. It wouldn't offer complete protection, but it was better than nothing.

As the outlaws drew closer, Elias mounted Buck, his movements swift but silent. The sorrel responded instantly, his powerful muscles bunching as he sensed the urgency of the moment. With a quiet word of encouragement, Elias urged Buck forward, guiding him toward the cleft in the rocks. The outlaws were now close enough to see him, but they didn't seem to have spotted the narrow passage he was aiming for.

He urged Buck on, the horse's hooves striking against the rocky ground, creating little sound against the backdrop of the wind whistling through the canyons. The outlaws yelled, spurred into action, their voices echoing through the darkening landscape. Elias pressed on, the ground beneath him rough and uneven, but Buck's powerful strides carried him swiftly over the obstacles.

They reached the cleft, a narrow opening that only allowed Buck's broad frame to pass. Elias guided his horse expertly through the rocky passage, heart pounding, and his grip tight on the reins. The outlaws followed, their shouts getting closer. Elias held his breath. He felt the horse's body brushing against the rough stone, their progress slowed by the narrowness of the passage. But they pressed on, inch by inch, inch by inch. He knew this would only buy them a small window, a moment, not salvation.

Emerging on the other side of the rocky passage, Elias found himself in a different part of the landscape, hidden from view. He didn't stop, didn't look back. He dared not even pause to assess his escape, urging his horse to run. They galloped through the twilight, the sounds of the outlaws' pursuit gradually fading behind them.

The escape had been a near thing, a brush with death that left him shaken but strangely exhilarated. He had narrowly escaped certain capture or worse. The incident underscored the harsh reality of his journey, a constant reminder of the danger that lurked in the shadows around every bend in the trail. He didn't know if they would attempt another approach or abandon their pursuit entirely.

He rode until the first light of dawn, finally finding a place to rest, exhausted but still alive. He didn't dare to build a fire, as the smoke might have betrayed his location. He simply rested, his senses heightened, his body still trembling from the adrenaline.

The encounter left an indelible mark on him, hardening his resolve and sharpening his instincts. He had faced the harsh reality of the frontier and survived. The journey was far from over, but this first brush with danger had taught him a valuable lesson: complacency was a deadly sin in the untamed West. He would press on, his steps lighter, his senses sharper, his determination burning even brighter. The memory of the outlaws' pursuit, the feel of Buck's powerful strides carrying him away from certain danger, served as a bitter reminder of what was at stake. The West was not just a beautiful and wild landscape but a perilous battleground where survival demanded constant vigilance and relentless courage.

The next few days were spent traveling cautiously, his eyes constantly scanning the horizon, his hand never far from his rifle. He adjusted his route, veering away from the trails he had previously planned to take. He sought out more remote paths, hoping to avoid further encounters with outlaws. He also began to pay closer attention to the signs of human activity, learning to recognize the subtle clues that could indicate the presence of other travelers, whether friendly or hostile. He even started to find a kind of grim satisfaction in the challenges, a sense of pride in his own resourcefulness and resilience. The frontier was testing him, pushing him to his limits, and he was meeting those challenges head-on, ready to face whatever dangers lay ahead. His determination was unshaken, his resolve strengthened by the adrenaline-fueled escape. The image of his sister remained his driving force, a beacon in the vast, unforgiving wilderness. He would reach Wyoming; he would find her. No matter the cost.

Chapter 4

Navigating Unfamiliar

Territory

The sun beat down mercilessly, turning the already parched earth into a shimmering mirage. Dust devils danced across the plains, swirling like miniature tornadoes, adding another layer of disorientation to Elias's already challenging journey. His body was so dehydrated that his lips were now as arid as the land around him. His body felt a crumbling ache upon it, his muscles giving up on him. Yet, the fire in his spirit seemed to be burning in the scorching sun.

He'd been riding for hours, the landscape unchanging—a monotonous expanse of scrub brush and rock formations under a sky that seemed to mock his thirst with its endless blue. His water skin was nearly empty, his tongue thick and swollen. The memory of cool Tennessee spring water, the feel of the damp earth beneath his bare feet back home, felt like a distant, almost unreal dream—a fantasy.

Man From Tennessee

He remembered the lush green fields of his family's farm, the comforting smell of freshly tilled soil, the comforting presence of family, a stark contrast to this desolate and unforgiving land. He could almost taste Mama's peach cobbler and feel the warmth of the hearth fire on a cold winter's night as he would sit by his window side and gaze into the open fields under the shining moon. The vividness of these memories only intensified the gnawing emptiness in his stomach and the burning dryness of his throat. He wasn't just battling the elements; he was battling the ghosts of his past, the loss of his home, and the uncertain future that stretched before him like an endless horizon.

The trail, barely discernible under the harsh sunlight, twisted and turned through canyons that seemed to swallow the light. He'd lost the familiar landmarks he'd been following, the faint tracks he'd been relying on now indistinguishable from the myriad of animal trails crisscrossing the land. He was utterly and completely lost, a terrifying realization in the vast emptiness of the Western plains. His compass, a cherished possession, had inexplicably failed, adding to the growing sense of despair.

Panic threatened to overwhelm him, but years of hard work on the farm had instilled in him a stubborn resilience. He fought back the rising fear, reminding himself of his sister, her hopeful smile, and her unwavering belief in his ability to find her. That image, the unwavering hope, became his lifeline, a flickering candle in the darkness. He pulled himself together, focusing on the immediate task: finding water and shelter before nightfall.

He dismounted Buck, the sorrel horse clearly showing the effects of the relentless heat and lack of water. The animal whinnied softly, its flanks heaving, its eyes reflecting the exhaustion of both beast and master. Elias knew that Buck's survival depended on him as much as his own. He had to find a way to make it through.

He spent hours searching, his eyes scanning every crevice and shadow, his body aching from the sun's unrelenting heat. Finally, he spotted a faint shimmer in the distance, a reflection of the setting sun on water. Hope surged through him, washing away some despair. He enthusiastically mounted Buck again, urging the weary animal forward once more.

The shimmer turned into a small, rocky stream, barely wider than his saddle, but its presence was a blessing. He allowed Buck to drink deeply, the thirsty animal gulping down the cool water with grateful sighs. Then, it was his turn. He cupped his hands, letting the life-giving liquid flow into his mouth, savoring each drop, the coolness of a balm to his parched throat.

The stream led him to a small, sheltered ravine, partially hidden by an overhang of rock. It wouldn't offer much protection from the elements, but it provided some respite from the relentless sun. He built a crude shelter with branches and brushwood to provide shade and protection from the wind. He then gathered firewood for the remaining daylight hours, carefully storing it close to his makeshift camp.

Night came swiftly in the vast expanse of the wilderness, the stars glittering like diamonds scattered across the velvet canvas of the night sky. The darkness in the sky was much more beautiful than the gloom on land. It seemed to be, albeit only temporarily, keeping all the murkiness at bay.

The cold night starkly contrasted the relentless heat of the day. The memories of Tennessee nights were even more vivid now, the warmth of the family home, the crackling fire in the hearth, far removed from the chill that penetrated his bones. He huddled close to his meager fire, the flames offering both warmth and psychological comfort, a reminder of life and humanity in this harsh and unforgiving landscape. He thought of his sister, visualizing her face in the dancing firelight, a beacon in his lonely vigil.

Navigating Unfamiliar Territory

The next few days were a repeat of the same arduous routine: endless stretches of barren land, intense heat, the constant threat of dehydration, the uncertainty of finding his way. But through it all, Elias persisted, driven by his unshakeable determination. He learned to read the subtle signs of the land, the wind's direction, and the sun's shadows, each a tiny clue helping him navigate the trackless wilderness. He learned to conserve his precious water, rationing each drop, using only what was absolutely necessary. He foraged for edible plants, and his knowledge of herbs and roots from his childhood in Tennessee proved invaluable.

One evening, as he was preparing his meager supper of roasted roots and berries, a sudden storm descended upon him, a furious tempest of wind and rain. The sky opened up, unleashing a torrent of water that turned the ravine into a rushing stream. He clung to the few possessions he'd managed to salvage, praying the storm would pass before the ravine filled entirely and swept him away. He fought against the deluge, bracing himself against the strong wind, his body battered by the wind and rain, his mind overwhelmed by the fury of nature. He had faced danger before, but this felt different, raw and visceral, a direct assault on his will to survive. The wind slapped him across the face, throwing him off-balance at will. It was too much for his weary body; he hadn't taken proper rest after last day's hustle.

The storm raged for hours, but as dawn approached, it finally began to subside. The rain ceased, and the wind calmed, leaving behind a landscape transformed—refreshed, revitalized, yet still formidable. He surveyed the damage: his shelter was wrecked, his firewood scattered, his clothes soaked, but he was alive. He started repairing what he could, and his resolve was unbent. The storm had tested him, but it hadn't broken him. He would continue; he would press on. His journey was far from over, but the resilience he had forged in these harsh conditions was a testament to the strength of his spirit, fueled by the thought of his sister and the promise of reunion. The West was a crucible, refining him, shaping him, making him stronger with every passing day, every challenge overcome.

The West was nothing like he had ever faced before. But then again, the West had never faced anyone like him before, as well.

Chapter 5
A Chance Encounter

The sun dipped below the horizon, painting the sky in fiery orange and deep purple hues. The storm, though having passed, left behind a damp chill that seeped into Elias's bones. He shivered, pulling his sodden shirt tighter around him. His meager fire sputtered, casting flickering shadows that danced across the ravaged landscape. He was physically and emotionally exhausted, yet the storm's adrenaline still coursed through his veins. He felt a strange mix of relief and apprehension, the quiet of the aftermath somehow more unsettling than the storm itself. It meant that something else was about to take the place of the vacuum that had been created.

As he sat there, lost in thought, a sound broke the silence—the distinct crackle of twigs underfoot, approaching steadily. Whoever, or whatever, was about to come out from behind the bush had Elias's undivided attention.

He did not turn around to face the uninvited guest, but he was tensed, his hand instinctively reaching for the makeshift knife he'd fashioned from a broken branch. He was wary, every instinct screaming caution in this unforgiving land where trust was a luxury few could afford. A figure emerged from the gathering dusk, silhouetted against the fading light.

The man was tall and gaunt, his face weathered like ancient bark, a thick beard framing a sharp gaze that seemed to pierce through the darkness. He carried himself with an easy confidence, the posture of a man accustomed to the harsh realities of the wilderness. A long rifle resting across his shoulders, its worn leather strap a testament to years of faithful service. His clothing was roughspun and patched but clean, suggesting a meticulous care that belied his rugged appearance.

"Evenin'," the man sarcastically greeted Elias, his voice a low rumble that seemed to blend with the sounds of the night. His accent was thick, a blend of mountain drawl and something else, something older, harder.

Elias, still cautious, slowly rose to his feet. Every movement calculated with his knife loosely held in his hand. "Evenin'," he greeted back, his voice hoarse from disuse and exertion.

A Chance Encounter

The stranger approached the fire, his eyes assessing Elias with a keen intelligence. He didn't appear hostile, but neither did he radiate warmth. There was a distance about him, a quiet intensity that hinted at a life lived on the edge.

"Name's Jedediah," the man said, extending a calloused hand.

Elias hesitated for a moment. Seemingly, he glanced at Jedidiah's propelled hand, but actually, he observed everything about the man from the front. His attire, what he was lacing. After a half-hearted contentment over the situation, he took the offered hand, feeling the strength of Jedediah in his grip. "Elias," he replied, his own hand dwarfed by the other man's.

Jedediah settled down beside the fire, pulling a worn leather pouch from his belt. He produced a small piece of dried meat and a chunk of hardtack, offering them to Elias. "Been a long day," he observed, his gaze fixed on the dancing flames.

Elias accepted the food gratefully. His rumbling stomach trumped pride and caution.

The food was plain, but it was nourishment, a welcome reprieve from the berries and roots that had been his staple for days. They ate in silence; the only sounds were the crackle of the fire and the chirping of unseen insects.

Man From Tennessee

As darkness deepened and the stars began appearing in the sky's vast expanse, Jedediah spoke. "You ain't from around here, son," he said, his voice barely a whisper. "That's plain to see."

Elias nodded. "Tennessee," he replied, the word carrying the weight of his loss, the longing for a life left behind.

Jedediah grunted, a sound of understanding. He knew the ache of leaving home, the pull of distant memories. He had seen it in countless faces and felt it in the lonely hearts who crossed his path.

"This land ain't for the faint of heart, I'll tell ya,' Jedediah said, his eyes scanning the star-strewn heavens. "It tests a man's soul, strips him bare, and leaves him only what he truly is." He paused, swirling the embers with a stick. "You'll find worse if you're heading West. Do yourself a favor and turn back."

Elias explained his quest, his search for his sister, Sarah, lost somewhere in the vastness of the unknown. He spoke of his escape from Tennessee, the burning hatred of his former employers, and the relentless pursuit that had forced him to flee. He detailed his perilous journey, his trials, and the determination that had driven him this far. He described Sarah, her kind eyes, her unwavering spirit.

Jedediah listened patiently, his gaze unwavering. When Elias finished, Jedediah was silent for a long moment, seemingly lost in thought, his eyes reflecting the distant stars.

"She's a strong one," Jedediah finally said, his voice still low and gravelly. "To have a brother like you, she's definitely got a fighting chance." He leaned closer, his voice dropping to an almost conspiratorial whisper. "But what I'm telling ya ain't just about getting across the plains. This land is full of dangers, dangers you can't even imagine. Outlaws, bandits... and much worse. "

He described the dangers in vivid detail—treacherous canyons, unpredictable weather, and the ever-present threat of hostile natives. He spoke of hidden trails, forgotten settlements, and places where law and order held little sway, some defy the concept entirely.

He warned Elias about the dangers of the unforgiving desert, the dwindling water sources, and the scorching sun. He recounted tales of lost souls, those who had succumbed to the relentless hardships of the Western frontier.

Man From Tennessee

"You'll need more than grit," Jedediah said, his gaze sharp and knowing. "You'll need luck and maybe... a little help from someone you don't expect." He paused, leaving Elias to ponder the meaning behind his cryptic warning.

Jedediah spoke of a hidden route, a seldom-used trail that could shave days off his journey, but it was a perilous path, fraught with danger. He offered Elias directions, crudely drawn on a piece of bark with charcoal. He shared his meager supplies, giving Elias additional food and a canteen of water. The man had grown a liking for Elias, like a brother Perhaps... a son.

He also gave Elias a warning that chilled him to the bone. He spoke of a ruthless gang known as the "Desert Dogs," who preyed upon travelers in the region, leaving no survivors.

Their notoriety for brutality was unheard of, their cruelty unmatched. Jedediah's description of their savagery sent shivers down Elias's spine, a stark reminder of the true danger he faced.

As dawn approached, casting a pale light across the landscape, Jedediah rose to his feet. "This is where our paths diverge," he said, a hint of something akin to sadness in his

A Chance Encounter

voice. "Remember what I told you. And keep your eyes open, son."

He disappeared into the predawn mist as quickly as he had appeared, leaving Elias alone by the fire's dying embers. He was left with the warmth of the shared fire, the memories of the shared food, and the weight of Jedediah's warnings, a burden of knowledge that weighed heavily upon his heart. The journey ahead was daunting, the dangers real and present, but he carried a newfound resolve. He had encountered a fellow traveler, a grizzled old mountain man. In that brief encounter, he had found crucial information and supplies and a renewed sense of hope—a testament to the unexpected connections that can be forged in the crucible of the wilderness. He was alone again, but he was no longer lost. He had found direction, not just on the map, but within himself. Jedidiah seemed to have been an angel sent to guide him, who was there for a moment but had priceless teachings to give.

Chapter 6
The Vastness of Wyoming

The Wyoming plains unfolded before Elias like a rumpled, sun-baked carpet stretching to the horizon. Gone were the familiar, comforting contours of the eastern woodlands.

The land was flat, vast, and utterly indifferent to his presence here. The wind, a constant companion, whispered secrets across the tall grasses, a sibilant language he didn't yet understand. The sun, a molten orb in the pale sky, beat down with merciless intensity, baking the earth to a hard, cracked crust. Each step sent a wave of heat radiating upwards, a physical manifestation of the challenge before him. His throat was already parched. The canteen Jedediah had given him feeling strangely inadequate against the scale of the thirst the landscape seemed to inspire.

The silence, broken only by the wind and the occasional cry of a hawk circling high above, was oppressive. It was a silence that pressed in on him, a physical weight amplifying his loneliness. The enormity of the prairie dwarfed him, making him feel insignificant, a tiny speck adrift in an ocean of grass.

Man From Tennessee

He was no longer merely traversing a landscape; he was navigating a psychological wilderness with challenges as immense as the physical terrain. He missed the comforting green of the trees, the familiar sounds of birdsong, the very feeling of shelter. This was a land of stark beauty and stark solitude.

The beauty, however, was undeniable. At sunrise and sunset, the sky blazed with colors too vibrant to be real—fiery oranges, molten yellows, and deep purples that bled into the night. Yet, in those colors' brilliance lurked quiet menace, reminding me how unforgiving the land can be. The vast expanse of the prairie shimmered with an ethereal quality, as if the land itself breathed, changing subtly with the shifting light. He'd seen such sunsets before, but never with such intensity or the same feeling of profound isolation. It was beautiful and, simultaneously, terrifyingly lonely.

The wildlife, too, was a constant reminder of nature's power. He saw pronghorn antelope, their sleek coats shimmering in the sunlight, disappearing into the sea of grass with breathtaking speed. He spotted coyotes, their thin, wiry bodies moving with an unsettling grace, their sharp cries echoing across the plains. Hearing their terrifying sounds, which echoed and trembled in the air as if in deathly retribution, it seemed to Vishwamitra harshly that he was an outsider amidst the tribal wolves of the wild. Once, he saw a lone bison, a magnificent creature, its massive frame a testament to the untamed nature of the land. The animal regarded him with an ancient, knowing gaze before slowly lumbering away, disappearing as quickly as it had appeared. While thrilling, these encounters were also a stark reminder of his vulnerability and the power of this unforgiving land.

Days bled into weeks; the journey was marked not by landmarks but by the relentless march of the sun and the slow, inexorable progress across the seemingly endless expanse. He meticulously rationed his food and water, the canteen becoming a precious burden, its weight a constant reminder of his dependence on its contents. The landscape shifted subtly but relentlessly, the grasses giving way to scrub brush, then to sparse, tenacious cacti clinging to the parched soil. The sun was a constant threat, its rays relentlessly beating down, drying his skin and making him feel weak and lethargic. Sleep was fitful, the vastness of the night sky, ablaze with stars, oddly unsettling, a reminder of how alone he was under the immensity of the heavens.

He fought against despair, fueled by the memory of Sarah's face and the burning need to find her. He pushed himself relentlessly, even as exhaustion gnawed at his resolve. He told himself that every step was a step closer, that each sunrise was a chance to find her. But the vastness of the plains worked its insidious magic, slowly eating away at his hope. It was a relentless test of his endurance, a challenge not only for his physical strength but also for his spirit.

One evening, a particularly violent thunderstorm swept across the plains. The wind howled like a banshee, whipping up the dry grass into a frenzy. Rain lashed down, briefly obscuring his vision. He huddled beneath a rocky outcrop, the cold seeping into his bones, the fear rising in his throat. The storm seemed to embody the savagery of the land, a brutal reminder of its power. When it finally subsided, he emerged, soaked to the bone but strangely exhilarated, as if the storm had cleansed him, purging him of his weariness and re-igniting a flicker of hope.

He found a small stream, its water cool and sweet, a welcome respite from the heat and the thirst that had been slowly tormenting him. He drank deeply, letting the water revive him, and then he washed his face, feeling the cool water revive his tired spirit. The stream was a gift, a small mercy in this desolate landscape, a symbol of hope in the vastness of the plains. It was a brief respite before he had to once again face the unrelenting horizon, which stretched toward a future that remained uncertain and far away. But even as he drank, he could not seem to rid the thought that the sweet moment of relief was only temporary and that the land was but granting him a brief intermission before it would test him again.

The loneliness, however, remained a constant companion. A subtle, insidious presence seeped into every aspect of his existence. He talked to himself, sometimes to Sarah's memory, sometimes just to maintain his sanity against the silence and the immensity of the vastness around him. It was a dialogue with himself, a way of maintaining some semblance of companionship. His solitude was a heavy shroud, a constant reminder that he was alone in this immense wilderness, a solitary figure in a land that demanded resilience and relentless courage.

The vastness of Wyoming was not just a physical challenge; it was a test of Elias's soul, a relentless examination of his fortitude. The solitude wasn't merely the absence of people but a profound isolation of spirit, a confrontation with the true limits of his resilience. He pressed onwards, driven not only by the hope of finding his sister but also by a desperate need to prove to himself that he was stronger than the immense challenges before him. The plains were a mirror to

Man From Tennessee

his own internal landscape, reflecting his fears, his hopes, and
the relentless determination that fueled his solitary journey
westward. His journey through Wyoming was a journey
inwards, a confrontation with himself and the limits of his
physical and spiritual strength. Each step was a victory, each
day survived was a testament to his resolve. And in the
relentless march westward, he found a strange solace, a quiet
strength forged in the crucible of the unforgiving Wyoming
plains. The vastness, though initially terrifying, eventually held
a subtle kind of beauty, a stark reminder of his own resilience,
a strength he would continue to draw upon in the harsh days
ahead.

Chapter 7
Tribal Encounters

The sun dipped below the horizon, painting the sky in hues of blood orange and bruised purple when Elias first saw them. A column of smoke, thin and grey against the fiery backdrop, rose from a hidden valley. His heart pounded a frantic rhythm against his ribs. He'd seen signs of other life—the tracks of deer, the scat of coyote, the fleeting glimpse of a pronghorn antelope—but this was different. This was deliberate, a sign of human habitation. A tribe.

Fear, cold and sharp, pierced through the growing chill of the evening. He'd heard stories, whispered tales around campfires back east, of savage tribes, of scalping and massacres. These stories, fueled by fear and prejudice, had painted a picture of merciless warriors, bloodthirsty and unforgiving. The reality, however, was far more nuanced, far more complex—standing on the edge of the unknown was a telltale for doom in the West.

He approached cautiously, his rifle held loosely at his side, more a symbol of preparedness than a weapon brandished in

39

aggression. The valley opened before him, revealing a village nestled amongst the rocky outcrops, a collection of tepees fashioned from tanned hides, smoke curling lazily from their tops. A few figures moved around, their silhouettes dark and indistinct against the fading light. The air hummed with a low, almost imperceptible sound, a murmur of voices that carried on the evening breeze.

Elias knew he couldn't simply walk in. He needed to make his intentions clear, to show he meant no harm. He chose a high vantage point, a rocky outcrop that offered a clear view of the village without exposing him to direct observation. He watched for a long time, studying their movements, their routines. He saw women tending to fires, children playing amongst themselves, and the rhythmic beat of a drum slowly pulsating in the fading light. It was a scene of peaceful domesticity that seemed strangely at odds with the fear that gripped him. A place of life, of order, and yet, the fear in his chest remained, a stubborn thing unwilling to loosen his grip.

The next morning, he approached more deliberately. He chose a spot where he was visible but not directly in their path, positioning himself near a small stream, showing that he was coming in peace, needing water, not invasion. He washed his face and hands openly, avoiding any sudden movements or any display of aggression. He knew that any sudden actions might spark fear and lead to immediate conflict. Patience was crucial; understanding their culture was pivotal.

It took several hours before anyone approached. A lone warrior emerged, his face painted with intricate designs, his eyes wary and assessing. He was tall and powerfully built, his physique honed by years spent living off the land. He carried a bow and arrow, his gaze never leaving Elias. The silence stretched between them, punctuated only by the gentle murmur of the stream. The bow in his hands was not raised, but neither was it lowered.

Elias offered a small gesture of peace—a slow raising of his hands, palms open, a universal sign of non-hostility. He spoke in English, his voice low and measured, knowing that the chances of understanding were slim. He accompanied his words with gestures, pointing to himself, then to the sun, then to the West, trying to convey his journey and his intentions. He pulled out a small, brightly colored piece of cloth, a scrap left over from his repairs, showing it as a sign of harmlessness. He reached into his bag and pulled out a little piece of brightly colored cloth—a harmless item, a token of goodwill. The cloth fluttered in the breeze as he extended it toward the warrior, his breath catching in his throat when the warrior's gaze flicked to it.

The warrior remained impassive, his expression unreadable. He studied Elias for a long moment, his eyes penetrating, searching. Then, slowly, he moved closer. He gestured for Elias to follow him, leading him back toward the village with a steady, unwavering gait. This gesture was a profound act of trust, a signal that he was willing to give the outsider a chance, albeit guarded. As it seemed, it was not an invitation. It was a test.

The village, up close, was more complex than it had first appeared. The tepees were arranged in a loose circle, with a central fire pit, suggesting a communal lifestyle. Children played near the outskirts, watching Elias with wide-eyed curiosity. Women were busy with various chores, their movements fluid and graceful. The atmosphere was one of guarded alertness but not outright hostility.

Elias was led to a larger tepee, where he was offered food—dried meat, berries, and a type of bread made from coarsely ground corn. He ate cautiously, aware that this gesture could be a test, a poisoned offering, but the food was plain and wholesome, seemingly devoid of malice. He made an effort to partake, understanding the importance of cultural acceptance as an act of respect. The warrior who had led him here watched him closely, his expression unreadable. Was he waiting for Elias to speak? Or to make a mistake?

Over the next few days, Elias's understanding of the tribe deepened. He learned that they were a band of Cheyenne, fiercely independent and proud of their heritage. They were skilled hunters and resourceful survivors intimately connected to the land and its rhythms. He learned some basic sign language, communicating through gestures and pointing, slowly bridging the linguistic gap. He discovered that their culture, far from being savage, was rich in traditions, complex in its social structures, and deeply spiritual in its outlook.

Misunderstandings remained. The Cheyenne had their own customs, traditions, and ways of interacting with outsiders. One particular incident highlighted this cultural difference.

Elias, used to his own way of personal space, sat too close to an elderly woman during a storytelling session, accidentally causing discomfort. Elias, out of habit, took a bowl before the elder had taken his share, earning him a sharp glance from the woman sitting beside him. The transgression was small, yet within that glance, he felt the weight of a lesson—of respect, hierarchy, and patience. The woman moved away subtly but firmly. It took a considerable amount of patient observing and gesturing before Elias understood the meaning of this respectful distance. He learned to be more mindful and observed carefully before action.

Elias, in turn, tried to share bits of his own culture, describing his life in the East, showing his worn leather-bound book, describing his sister, and explaining his journey. He drew pictures in the dust using a stick to illustrate certain aspects of his life and the purpose of his travels. Though it was a crude translation, it was a sincere effort to build trust and connect on a human level, irrespective of language barriers.

As the days turned into weeks, a tentative alliance began to form. The initial fear and suspicion started to ease, replaced by a cautious curiosity and then slowly growing respect. He was never fully accepted, never fully integrated into their way of life, but he was tolerated. He was a stranger, an outsider, but he had shown respect and acted with caution. They recognized that this "pale face" was different, that his intentions, despite the inherent threat of his presence, seemed genuine.

The tribe's wisdom and understanding of the land taught Elias much-needed lessons. He learned to recognize the subtle signs of the prairie, the language of wind and sky, and the patterns of wildlife. He learned to respect the delicate balance of the ecosystem. The Cheyenne were not just inhabitants of the land; they were part of it, inextricably linked to its rhythms and its cycles. He realized that survival here was not about conquest, it was about harmony.

His time with the Cheyenne tribe was a profound learning experience. It taught him humility, the limitations of his own perspective, and the importance of intercultural understanding. His initial fear was replaced by a deep respect for a vastly different culture. He left the tribe not as a conquering outside but as a traveler who had learned a valuable lesson: sometimes, the most formidable challenges are met not with aggression but with patience, respect, and understanding. The journey west continued, but Elias was no longer the same man who had first entered the shadow of the plains. He carried with him the wisdom of the Cheyenne, a knowledge that would serve him well in the challenging days that lay ahead. The echoes of their drums, the scent of their campfires, and the memory of their quiet dignity would remain with him as a constant reminder of the human capacity for both suspicion and understanding, for fear and compassion. The journey westward was not only a quest to find his sister but a journey of self-discovery, a path that had led him to an unexpected yet invaluable understanding of himself and the vast and varied nature of humanity.

He had come searching for his sister, but in this village, he had found a small measure of peace.

Chapter 8
Survival on the Plains

The sun beat down relentlessly, a hammer forging the plains into a shimmering, heat-hazed expanse. Days bled into one another; each marked only by the relentless march of the sun across the sky and the gnawing emptiness in Elias's stomach.

The Cheyenne, generous as they had been, were not a limitless resource. He had been permitted to hunt with them, to learn their ways, but the time had come to continue his journey westward, alone once more.

Water became his immediate obsession. The streams he'd found near the Cheyenne village were now distant memories, swallowed by the vast, thirsty land. Once brimming with cool water, his canteen was now a dry, parched shell, a mocking reminder of his dwindling reserves. Each swallow of air seared his throat, his tongue thick and useless against the creeping thirst.

Man From Tennessee

He searched for hours, his throat constricting, his vision blurring under the relentless sun. Once a source of fascination, the landscape was now a cruel adversary, offering little respite from the burning heat. Each step felt like an agonizing effort, his boots sinking slightly into the parched earth, a testament to the relentless dryness.

His knowledge of nature, honed through countless hours spent studying books and observing the natural world, became his lifeline. He remembered passages from old texts describing how to locate water sources in arid environments. He searched for signs—the subtle dip in the land, the slightly greener hue of vegetation, the gathering of birds near a hidden spring. Each clue sparked hope, only for disappointment to follow when the earth remained dry—cracked and lifeless. He followed the flight patterns of vultures, knowing that their circling often indicated a source of carrion and nearby, perhaps a source of water. It was a slow, painstaking process, filled with false hopes and crushing disappointments. Days turned into a relentless cycle of searching, hoping, and despair.

It was like a miracle when he finally stumbled upon a small, almost imperceptible seep of water. The water was barely a trickle, muddy and tinged with minerals, but it was life itself. He cupped his hands, greedily lapping up the precious liquid, feeling the cool moisture revive his parched throat. He drank slowly, savoring each drop, aware that this small source of water was a fleeting gift in the harsh desert. He filled his canteen, carefully rationing his supply, knowing that this might be the only water he'd encounter for many days.

Food was another formidable challenge. The game, once plentiful near the Cheyenne village, was now scarce. His hunting skills, though honed, were insufficient to provide him with a reliable supply of sustenance. He spent days tracking rabbits and prairie dogs, his movements slow and deliberate, his eyes constantly scanning the horizon. The animals, wary and agile, were difficult to catch. More than once, he raised his rifle only to have his prey dart away at the last second, leaving him cursing into the vast emptiness. He learned to stalk them patiently, using the shadows and the uneven terrain to his advantage. Many hunts ended in failure, leaving him with nothing but aching muscles and an even emptier stomach.

Hunger gnawed at him relentlessly, a constant companion that tested his physical and mental fortitude. He learned to recognize edible plants, and his knowledge of botany proved unexpectedly useful. He identified cacti, roots, and berries, cautiously sampling each one, aware of the dangers of consuming poisonous vegetation. He learned to distinguish between the palatable and the toxic; his survival depended on his ability to differentiate between the two. His diet became meager and monotonous, consisting mostly of bitter roots and tasteless berries. The pangs in his stomach never truly faded, only dulled into a constant ache.

The sun continued to be his implacable enemy. The days were unbearably hot, baking the land into an infertile wasteland. The nights offered little respite, the temperatures dropping sharply, bringing with them a bone-chilling cold.

Elias sought shelter wherever he could find it—under the sparse shade of scrubby bushes, in shallow rock crevices, or behind the meager protection of large rocks. His clothing, once pristine, was now ragged and torn, bearing witness to the harshness of his ordeal. His body, too, bore the marks of his struggle—sunburnt skin, blistered hands, and cracked lips.

One night, a fierce sandstorm descended upon him, burying him under a mountain of sand and debris. He fought desperately to breathe, his lungs filling with sand, his eyes stinging with pain. He felt like he was suffocating, his body battered by the relentless wind. When the storm finally subsided, he emerged weak and disoriented, his clothes torn, his body covered in sand. He felt defeated, his spirit broken, but the primal instinct to survive pushed him onward.

Survival on the Plains

He discovered that even in the most desolate landscapes, life found a way. He observed the creatures of the plains—the ants, the beetles, the lizards—finding inspiration in their tenacity and adaptability. He learned from them, mimicking their resourcefulness and emulating their ability to withstand the seemingly insurmountable challenges of the harsh environment.

Despite the hardships, he also found moments of quiet beauty. The sunrise, casting a golden hue over the vast expanse of the plains, was a breathtaking spectacle. The clear, starry nights, devoid of city lights, revealed a breathtaking celestial panorama. For all its cruelty, the land was still beautiful, and in that beauty, he found a reason to keep going. These moments of beauty served as reminders of the enduring power of nature and its capacity to inspire even in the face of adversity.

His journey across the plains was not merely a physical ordeal but a crucible that tested his spirit, resilience, and determination. He emerged, changed by the experience, hardened and humbled; his faith in his own abilities strengthened, his respect for the power of nature deepened, and his understanding of the human capacity for perseverance profoundly altered. The plains had stripped him bare, but it had also revealed the incredible strength and resilience of the

Man From Tennessee

human spirit, a strength that he never knew he possessed until he was pushed to his absolute limits. The journey westward continued, but the plains had become more than just a challenge to overcome; it had become a test of survival, both physical and spiritual, that transformed him in ways he could never have anticipated.

Chapter 9

A Desperate Alliance

The setting sun cast long, skeletal shadows across the parched earth, painting the landscape in hues of orange and purple. Elias, his body leaner, his face etched with the harsh realities of his journey, sat huddled beneath a scraggly mesquite bush, nursing a meager portion of water. His canteen, though replenished at that fortuitous seep, was again dwindling. The unforgiving and vast land stretched before him, a seemingly endless expanse of dust and rock.

Despair, a familiar companion, threatened to engulf him once more.

Just as he was surrendering to the crushing weight of hopelessness, a sound broke the stillness—the soft thud of hooves on the dry earth, barely audible above the whisper of the wind. He tensed, his hand instinctively reaching for the worn hunting knife at his belt. He had seen few other humans since leaving the Cheyenne village, and those encounters had been infrequent and often unsettling.

Man From Tennessee

Out of the gathering dusk emerged a lone figure silhouetted against the fiery horizon. The rider moved with quiet confidence, each shift in the saddle deliberate, controlled. A Native American, his face obscured by the shadow of his wide-brimmed hat, rode a powerfully built mustang, its coat the color of burnt umber. The scout's attire was simple yet practical: worn leather trousers, a buckskin shirt, and a blanket draped over his saddle. He carried a long rifle across his lap, the barrel gleaming faintly in the fading light.

He halted a short distance away, observing Elias with a keen, assessing gaze. Silence hung heavy between them, broken only by the rustling of the wind through the sparse vegetation. Elias, despite his exhaustion and hunger, felt a surge of apprehension. His heart pounded, his body screaming at him to act—run, fight, do something—but he forced himself to stay calm. He had learned to respect the inherent caution of the plains people, their keen awareness of the dangers hidden within the seemingly empty landscape.

Finally, the scout spoke, his voice low and gravelly, laced with the accent of the plains. His words were in a language Elias didn't understand, yet the tone conveyed a mixture of suspicion and curiosity. Each syllable was measured and probed for more.

A Desperate Alliance

Having learned a few basic phrases from his time with the Cheyenne, Elias attempted a greeting in their language, but his pronunciation was rough and hesitant.

The scout responded, though not in Cheyenne. His words were in a different dialect, perhaps Kiowa or Comanche. Elias couldn't be certain. He could only make out a few words, and the gist seemed to be a question about Elias's purpose on the plains, tinged with an underlying skepticism.

Speaking slowly and carefully in English, Elias explained his situation—his journey westward, his desperate need for water and supplies, and his hardships. He spoke of his respect for the indigenous peoples of the land, hoping to establish a bridge of understanding rather than create conflict. He knew the dangers of appearing threatening or presumptuous in this harsh and unpredictable land.

The scout listened patiently, his eyes never leaving Elias. After Elias finished his explanation, a long silence stretched between them. The scout scrutinized him for what felt like an eternity, evaluating his words and his demeanor, perhaps even sensing his desperation. Finally, the scout spoke again, his voice still low but with a hint of grudging respect. He offered Elias a gesture—a slight nod of his head, almost imperceptible in the fading light—an indication of willingness to assist.

Man From Tennessee

The journey forward was slow and arduous, marked by the challenges of the terrain and the unspoken tension between the two men. The scout, whose name Elias learned was Kiowa, remained taciturn, revealing little about himself. His knowledge of the land, however, was undeniable. He seemed to possess an almost supernatural ability to navigate the treacherous landscape, leading Elias to hidden springs and trails known only to those who lived intimately with the land. Every movement he made was intentional as if he could feel the earth beneath his feet. Though not a religious man, the scout made Elias think about a higher power.

Their alliance was fragile, built on mutual need rather than genuine trust. Elias depended on Kiowa's guidance but remained wary of the scout's true motives. He knew trust in this land was a currency, one not given freely.

Kiowa, in turn, seemed reluctant to divulge too much, always maintaining a careful distance, a watchful eye scanning the horizon for any sign of danger. His silence was not rudeness—it was survival.

One evening, as they rested beside a small creek, the silence between them was punctuated by the crackling of the fire.

A Desperate Alliance

Elias, emboldened by a shared meal of roasted rabbit,
attempted to learn more about Kiowa. He asked about his tribe
and his life on the plains, hoping to bridge the cultural divide
that separated them. The question lingered in the air like a
delicate thing that easily can be shattered.

Kiowa, initially resistant, slowly began to open up. He
spoke of the encroaching settlements of the white man, the loss
of ancestral lands, and the constant threat of violence and
displacement. His voice was filled with a quiet sadness, a sense
of loss that mirrored Elias's own feelings of displacement and
loneliness. He spoke of the importance of preserving his
people's way of life, their deep connection to the land, and their
intricate understanding of its rhythms and its secrets.

Elias, in turn, shared his story, reasons for traveling west,
hopes, and fears. He spoke of the injustices he had witnessed,
the greed and violence that drove so many westward, and his
desire to build a better future, a future where different cultures
could coexist peacefully. He spoke of his connection to the land,
recognizing its character's beauty and harshness.

As they talked, a bond of sorts began to form, a tenuous
link forged in the crucible of shared adversity. They were two
men from vastly different worlds, their cultures separated by
centuries of history and vast differences in custom, yet they

shared a common thread—the struggle for survival in a land that demanded both resilience and adaptability. Trust, though fragile, had begun to take root.

The distant howls of coyotes often punctuated their nights, the mournful cries echoing through the silent plains, and the crackle of their small campfire, a fragile beacon against the immensity of the night sky. The days were spent navigating the labyrinthine canyons and windswept mesas, avoiding the treacherous ravines and waterless stretches.

Each step was a victory against the odds, and each shared hardship brought them closer. Yet, in the shadows, uncertainty lurked.

Their interactions were a delicate dance between two cultures, a tacit acknowledgment of their differences balanced by the common goal of survival. The tension between them was always present, a quiet undercurrent to their strained alliance. But as the days turned into weeks, a grudging respect developed, a hesitant trust slowly taking root in the barren soil of their circumstances. The land had tested them both, but neither had faltered. At least, not yet.

Their journey together, however difficult, was a testament to the unexpected alliances that can be formed in the face of

A Desperate Alliance

shared adversity. Once a daunting and hostile environment, the plains began to feel slightly less menacing, the vastness slightly less lonely. They were no longer just two individuals struggling alone but a temporary team bound by a fragile hope of reaching their destination. However, the West remained a mysterious and unforgiving realm, full of unpredictable threats hidden beneath the seemingly empty sky. The alliance, while beneficial, was fragile, and the challenges yet to come would surely test the bounds of their uneasy partnership. Far from over, the journey was still fraught with danger and uncertainty.

For now, they rode on together, bound not by friendship but by necessity. Bound by interest and a need for a partner, onward the two men rode.

Chapter 10

The Pursuit Begins

The rhythmic thud of hooves, once a source of tentative hope, now echoed with a sinister urgency. The distant dust, initially a mirage in the shimmering heat, solidified into a menacing cloud on the horizon, growing larger with each passing moment. His usually impassive face etched with grim determination, Kiowa urged his mustang forward, and his gaze fixed on the approaching threat. The tranquility of their journey had shattered; the pursuit had begun.

Three figures, dark silhouettes against the pale sky, emerged from the dust cloud, their forms gradually resolving into a trio of riders. Outlaws. Elias recognized the shape of their Winchester rifles, the glint of sunlight on their polished barrels a chilling testament to their lethal intent. The air crackled with unspoken menace, the silence broken only by the pounding of hooves and the frantic beat of Elias's own heart.

He had unknowingly stumbled into a hornet's nest. Days before, his encounter with the prospector, Silas—a fleeting, almost inconsequential meeting—had apparently been reported to these merciless men. It seemed Silas was not one to remain silent when the opportunity for profit presented itself. Elias's possession of the map, the prospector's desperate greed, and a trail of unwitting clues—these all had combined to put a reward on Elias's head.

Kiowa, sensing the desperation in Elias's eyes, didn't need words. He understood. The unspoken understanding between them, forged in shared hardship, transformed into a fierce determination. Their uneasy alliance had become a necessity, a matter of survival against overwhelming odds. The vastness of the plains, once a symbol of solitude, had become a hunting ground, the endless horizon a relentless reminder of the pursuers closing in.

The chase became a blur of motion, a chaotic ballet of dust and desperation. With his intimate knowledge of the land, Kiowa skillfully guided them through treacherous canyons and across unforgiving stretches of desert. His mastery of the terrain bought them precious time, but it was a constant race against the relentless advance of the outlaws. Their horses spurred to their limits, strained against the relentless pressure, their breath coming in ragged gasps.

The outlaws were ruthless, exhibiting no mercy. Their shots, aimed with deadly precision, ripped through the air, whistling past them with chilling proximity. Each bullet was a stark reminder of their vulnerability, the fragility of their fragile alliance. While offering some protection, the terrain also presented its own dangers, forcing Kiowa to make daring maneuvers, navigating narrow passages and steep inclines.

Clinging to the saddle, Elias felt the raw power of the mustang beneath him, its muscles rippling with exertion. The wind whipped through his hair, carrying with it the smell of dust and the metallic scent of fear. His own horse, though slower, remained surprisingly steadfast, its endurance a testament to its resilience. His own body ached, his muscles screaming in protest, but the thought of his sister—her image a beacon of hope in the storm of his fear—pushed him onward.

The outlaws, clearly experienced and relentless in their pursuit, were not merely trying to capture him; they seemed intent on eliminating him. Their shots grew more frequent and more accurate, leaving Elias and Kiowa with increasingly fewer options for escape. Twice, they narrowly avoided being trapped in blind alleys, only Kiowa's sharp eye and instinctive knowledge of the terrain preventing them from falling into ambushes.

The sun beat down mercilessly, turning the landscape into an oven. The heat added another layer of torment to the already grueling chase, dehydrating them and pushing their endurance to its limits. The scant water they had managed to salvage from hidden springs was dwindling, and thirst added to their already mounting despair.

As the day wore on, the chase became more of a desperate struggle for survival. The outlaws, fueled by greed and a thirst for blood, pressed their advantage relentlessly, their determination unwavering. The landscape, once a neutral participant, now seemed to conspire against them, its harsh realities constantly threatening to end their desperate flight.

Nightfall brought a semblance of respite, but it also introduced new dangers. The darkness masked their movements, making the terrain even more treacherous. However, it also offered some measure of concealment, a tactical advantage that Kiowa deftly utilized.

The pursuit continued through the night, an arduous, exhausting, and relentless struggle against the odds. They found temporary refuge in rocky crevices and shadowy canyons, resting briefly, the air filled with the rustling of the wind, the distant howls of coyotes, and the ever-present threat of discovery. Sleep offered little respite, and the constant fear of being discovered kept them on edge.

The Pursuit Begins

The bond between Elias and Kiowa had strengthened, forged in the crucible of their shared danger. Words were sparse, and their communication consisted mainly of gestures and unspoken understanding. Each silent act of trust, each shared glance, reaffirmed their uneasy alliance, a fragile thread binding them together in their desperate fight for survival.

With the dawn of a new day, the pursuit resumed the chase once again, becoming a blur of movement and desperation. Elias's resolve, fueled by a fierce determination to reach safety and protect his sister, remained unbroken. The outlaws, undeterred, maintained their relentless pressure, their presence a constant reminder of the mortal danger that lurked just beyond the horizon.

The landscape offered little comfort, the barren plains offering no respite. Each rise, each dip, each twist of the trail was a gamble, a test of their skill and endurance. The tension was palpable. A silent scream held captive within the confines of their perilous journey. The relentless pounding of the horses' hooves, the rasp of their breathing, and the echo of gunshots punctuated the silence, a symphony of survival and dread. The pursuit was a harsh master, pushing them to their limits and threatening to extinguish their hopes before they could ever reach their destination.

Man From Tennessee

The relentless chase continued a brutal test of their endurance and will, a relentless pressure that seemed designed to break them. But Elias and Kiowa, bound by the need for survival, pushed onward, their determination hardened by the stark realities of their predicament. The plains, once a vast and empty expanse, now felt claustrophobic, the horizon a looming threat rather than a promise of freedom. The outlaws were relentless, but so was their will to survive. Their journey, far from over, was a testament to human endurance, a grim dance between life and death on the unforgiving landscape of the American West. The pursuit was relentless, but so was their hope. The destination remained elusive, but the will to survive remained stronger. The journey continued...

Chapter 11
Entering the Mountains

The plains gave way to the foothills, a gradual ascent that soon turned brutally steep. The rhythmic pounding of hooves against the hard-packed earth of the plains was replaced by the jarring clatter of rocks and the skittering of loose shale under their mounts' hooves. Kiowa, his bronzed face grimmer than ever, expertly navigated the treacherous trail, his knowledge of these mountains as profound as his understanding of the plains. Elias, clinging precariously to his saddle, felt a raw, primal fear grip his heart. The vastness of the sky, once a symbol of hope, now seemed to press down, the towering peaks above threatening to crush them.

The air thinned with each upward turn of the trail, the familiar heat of the lowlands replaced by a biting chill that snaked into their bones. The sun, a malevolent eye in the vast sky, beat down with relentless intensity, yet the wind carried a sharp, icy bite. This was a land of extremes, a testament to nature's brutal indifference. Elias accustomed to the familiar heat of the desert, shivered, his breath misting in the frigid air.

Man From Tennessee

The path became a tortuous labyrinth, a winding ribbon of rock and earth snaking through a landscape of jagged peaks and deep, shadowed canyons. The ascent was a brutal test of their horses' endurance, each step a struggle against the unforgiving terrain. The animals, their flanks heaving, their breath coming in ragged gasps, responded to Kiowa's silent commands with a desperate loyalty, their instinctual understanding of the dangers a vital part of their survival.

The sheer cliffs and precipitous drops presented a constant threat, the slightest misstep capable of sending them tumbling into the unforgiving abyss below. Elias, his hands raw and bleeding from gripping the reins, felt a gnawing anxiety in the pit of his stomach. Though seemingly lost in the sprawling expanse of the foothills, the outlaws might reappear at any moment, their deadly accuracy made all the more dangerous by the unforgiving terrain.

Despite the physical demands of the ascent, Kiowa seemed unfazed, his movements fluid and precise. He possessed an uncanny ability to find the best route, selecting paths that minimized risk while maximizing speed. His knowledge of the hidden trails and concealed passages was astounding, a testament to years spent traversing these unforgiving mountains. He seemed to sense the shifts in the weather, the

Entering the Mountains

subtle changes in temperature and wind, predicting potential hazards before they arose. His intuition was as vital as his physical skill.

The unpredictable and harsh weather added another layer of complexity to their perilous journey. The sun, a merciless tyrant in the high country, could vanish behind a curtain of snow-laden clouds in the blink of an eye, unleashing a sudden, chilling blizzard that obscured the trail and threatened to overwhelm them. Unprepared for the sudden change in temperature, Elias shivered uncontrollably, his thin clothing offering little protection against the biting wind. He had to fight to stay on his horse as the wind threatened to blow them off the narrow path.

The landscape offered little respite, its harsh beauty both mesmerizing and intimidating. The towering peaks, cloaked in snow and ice, stood like silent sentinels, their majestic forms a chilling reminder of nature's immense power. The deep canyons, shrouded in shadow, were filled with an ominous silence, their depths concealing unseen dangers.

The wind howled through the mountain passes, carrying with it the scent of snow and the chilling whisper of the unknown.

Man From Tennessee

Elias, his body aching, his lungs burning, fought to suppress the rising panic. The thin air made each breath laborious, his heart pounding a frantic rhythm against his ribs.

He struggled to keep his focus, his mind battling against the insidious creep of exhaustion and fear. The pursuit weighed heavily upon him, its unrelenting pressure a constant drain on his physical and mental resources.

But despite the overwhelming odds, Elias found a strange solace in the solitude of the mountains. The relentless chase and the constant threat of the outlaws seemed momentarily forgotten amidst the vastness of the landscape. The majesty of the mountains, their silent strength, provided a sense of perspective, a humbling reminder of the insignificance of human conflicts in the face of nature's immensity.

Kiowa, sensing Elias's distress, offered a brief, reassuring smile. It was a small gesture, but it spoke volumes of the unspoken bond that had formed between them. Their differences, once so stark, seemed to fade into insignificance amidst the shared dangers of their perilous journey. In a sense, they were united by a desperate need for survival. Though treacherous and unforgiving, the mountains had forged a strange camaraderie between these two unlikely allies.

Entering the Mountains

The descent proved as treacherous as the ascent. The loose rocks and uneven terrain challenged their skill and endurance. Each misstep was a gamble, a potential catastrophe waiting to happen. Elias's muscles, strained from the climb, screamed in protest, yet he pressed onward, the image of his sister his driving force. He had to get to her, and he had to protect her. That thought, that unwavering determination, was his strength, his shield against the unrelenting onslaught of exhaustion and fear.

They found temporary shelter in a narrow crevice, shielded from the wind and the biting cold. Kiowa built a small fire, the flames dancing and flickering against the cold stone walls, offering a fragile warmth against the gathering darkness. Elias, wrapped in a thin blanket, drank some of their dwindling water, feeling the life slowly returning to his chilled limbs. The silence was broken only by the crackling fire and the distant howl of the wind.

Rest was fleeting, the constant vigilance necessary for survival allowing little more than a few hours of fitful sleep. They were always alert, aware of the potential dangers that lurked in the shadows, and the precariousness of their position was a stark reminder of their vulnerability. The mountains offered no easy solutions, no simple escape. Their journey was a brutal test, a trial of both endurance and cunning

As dawn broke, they continued their descent, each step a cautious maneuver, each turn of the trail a gamble. The terrain was less steep but still treacherous, and the ground was uneven and treacherous underfoot. Their weary but resilient horses carried them through the rocky terrain, their loyalty a testament to their indomitable spirit. The outlaws remained a constant threat, a silent presence lurking in the shadows, their absence as ominous as their potential reappearance.

As the mountains finally gave way to the valley below, a sense of relief washed over Elias. The vast expanse of the plains offered a different kind of danger, but it was a danger he knew, a danger he could perhaps contend with. The treacherous mountains, however, had tested him to his limits, pushing him to the brink of despair but ultimately revealing the strength of his spirit. The journey had been arduous—a crucible that had forged a new resolve within him, a fiercer determination to reach his destination and claim his freedom. But the journey was far from over, the road to safety still long and fraught with peril. The escape from the mountains was a victory, but the battle for survival was far from won.

Chapter 12

Mountain Ambush

The valley floor, a deceptive respite after the brutal climb, offered little solace. The relative flatness was a cruel trick of the eye; the terrain remained treacherous, a patchwork of jagged rocks and hidden ravines. As they rode, a prickling unease settled over Elias. The silence, once a welcome change from the howling wind of the mountains, now felt oppressive, heavy with unspoken threat. Kiowa, usually so stoic, seemed tense, his eyes constantly scanning the surrounding landscape, his hand never far from the hilt of his knife.

Still thin and biting, the air carried the faint scent of woodsmoke, a jarring note in the otherwise pristine wilderness. It was a scent that spoke of human presence, of habitation, but not the kind that offered refuge. Elias's gut clenched. He knew, with a chilling certainty, that their respite was over.

The ambush came without warning, a sudden eruption of violence that shattered the deceptive calm. From behind a cluster of boulders, a ragged band of outlaws emerged, their faces masked by shadows and dust, their eyes glinting with a predatory gleam. Their numbers were greater than Elias had anticipated, at least a dozen men, their horses equally as hardy as their own, their weapons gleaming menacingly in the afternoon sun.

The narrowness of the pass, a seemingly safe haven moments before, now proved to be their deadliest trap. There was no room to maneuver, no space to escape. They were pinned, surrounded on three sides by the relentless advance of the outlaws. The fourth side, a sheer cliff face, offered no possibility of escape.

The outlaws, fueled by a brutal mix of desperation and greed, charged, a chaotic wave of gunfire and shouts erupting as they unleashed a volley of shots. Elias reacted instinctively, drawing his own pistol and returning fire, the sharp crack of the weapon momentarily drowning out the roar of the assault. His shots found their mark, two outlaws slumping to the ground, but the relentless barrage continued. Bullets whistled past his head, sending rocks skittering down the canyon walls.

Kiowa, meanwhile, was a whirlwind of motion, his movements fluid and deadly. He didn't waste time firing his own weapon; instead, he used his knife with terrifying efficiency, deflecting bullets with incredible dexterity and slicing through the air with deadly accuracy. He was a phantom, a blur of motion that seemed to be everywhere at once, a living embodiment of the unforgiving wilderness they had just traversed.

The fight was brutal, a desperate struggle for survival waged in the heart of a claustrophobic canyon. Elias fought back with a ferocity he didn't know he possessed, his desperation fueling his every move. He rolled away from a stray bullet, and, using the ground as cover, he scrambled toward a larger boulder, seeking a more defensible position. He could hear the enraged shouts of the outlaws, their relentless pursuit echoing around him.

The intensity of the confrontation was staggering: the clash of steel against steel, the deafening reports of gunfire, and the pained groans of wounded men—all set against the dramatic backdrop of the towering mountain peaks. The air hung thick with the smell of gunpowder and sweat, the taste of dust and blood coating Elias's tongue.

His initial supply of ammunition dwindled rapidly. He dropped his empty pistol, grasping for a spare weapon at his saddle. Meanwhile, despite being outnumbered, Kiowa seemed to hold his own, a silent, deadly force against the tide of violence. He moved with an almost supernatural agility, his knife flashing like lightning, each strike precise and deadly.

Elias, finding a slight opening, unleashed a flurry of punches and kicks, knocking an outlaw to the ground and seizing the man's rifle in the process. He raised the rifle, took aim, and shot. He felt a surge of adrenaline as his shot struck the outlaw's chest, bringing the man down. He was fighting for his life—the raw, primal energy of survival coursed through him.

He was running out of time, though. More outlaws were closing in, their intent to overwhelm them with sheer force. Kiowa, sensing their desperation, gave a sharp shout, drawing the attention of several of the outlaws. He used that distraction, sprinting toward a nearby thicket, signaling Elias to follow. His body screamed in protest, and Elias pushed his weary body, sprinting along with Kiowa.

Their escape was narrow. Several shots whizzed past them, some grazing Elias's clothes. He could feel the stinging sensation on his skin. He didn't dare look back. But they were faster; their years of riding through these mountains gave them an edge, an understanding of the terrain that allowed them to navigate through the dense undergrowth while the thicket slacked the outlaws.

They burst from the undergrowth, gasping for breath, onto a somewhat clearer section of the valley. They had bought themselves some time, a precious few minutes, to regain their breath and assess their situation. Their pursuers were close behind, though. They didn't have much time.

They could hear the outlaws' shouting, echoing through the valley. They turned and saw them, and they spurred their horses onward, the rocky terrain now an obstacle but not a barrier. They were not letting them catch them. They had to escape.

Their mounts responded instinctively, pushing themselves to their limits. Their hearts pounded in their chests, matching the rhythm of their horses' pounding hooves. They had to get away. Their survival depended on it.

The chase continued the relentless pursuit of a desperate race against time. The outlaws were tenacious, fueled by the anger of their failed ambush. Their shots still rang out, but Elias and Kiowa skillfully avoided the attacks; their movements synchronized, and their bond solidified in the crucible of battle.

Man From Tennessee

After what seemed like an eternity, they reached a more open area, a vast expanse of plain that promised a chance at escape. The mountains receded behind them, their menacing peaks now distant silhouettes against the setting sun. They had won this battle.

But as they looked back, they realized the outlaws had abandoned their pursuit. They were safe, for now. They had survived. But the escape from the mountains had left them wounded, both physically and emotionally. The scars of the ambush would take time to heal. But they had survived. And that was everything. Their journey was far from over, but they had survived a deadly ambush.

And so... onward they tread.

Chapter 13
A Narrow Escape

The horses, sensing the urgency in their riders' desperation, responded with a raw, primal energy of their own. Their muscles bunched, their breath coming in ragged gasps, but they ran. They ran as if their very lives depended on it, which, of course, they did. The ground blurred beneath their hooves—a chaotic jumble of rocks, loose soil, and sparse scrub. Elias, clinging to his saddle, felt the jarring impact of each uneven stride, his body screaming in protest, but his will was stronger. He had to keep going.

Kiowa, ever watchful, guided them instinctively through the treacherous terrain. He knew these mountains like the back of his hand, his knowledge of hidden trails and precarious paths proving invaluable in their desperate flight. He was a maestro conducting a symphony of survival, his every movement precise and deliberate, leading them away from the pursuing outlaws with a skill honed by years of navigating the unforgiving landscape.

Man From Tennessee

The rhythmic pounding of their horse's hooves was a relentless drumbeat against the backdrop of the outlaws' increasingly distant shouts. The sounds echoed through the valley, fading into the distance but still close enough to fuel their desperate flight. Every now and then, a stray bullet would whiz past, the sound a chilling reminder of the danger that still lurked behind them.

Elias, his senses heightened by the adrenaline coursing through his veins, noticed a subtle shift in the terrain. The valley floor began to open up, the dense undergrowth thinning, giving way to a wider expanse. Hope, a fragile ember, flickered within him. Perhaps, just perhaps, they might yet escape.

They reached a shallow river, its waters rushing swiftly toward a wider valley. The outlaws would be slowed, their horses hesitant to cross the turbulent current, but the river posed its own risks. A miscalculation could lead to a fatal plunge, the cold, swift water dragging them down into a watery grave.

Kiowa, his eyes scanning the riverbank, spotted a narrow, precarious ford. It was a risky option; the rocks were slippery, and the current was strong, but it offered their best chance of escape. He urged his horse toward the crossing. Elias, mimicking his movements, followed, the water splashing up around them, threatening to unseat them at any moment.

The crossing was a test of skill and nerve, a perilous dance on the edge of disaster. But they made it. The riverbank on the far side offered a moment's respite. They pulled their horses to a halt, their bodies trembling with exhaustion, their lungs burning from the exertion. They had made it for now.

As they emerged onto the wider valley, their pursuers were still visible, but the distance between them had widened significantly. The outlaws, hampered by the river crossing, were falling behind. Elias felt a surge of relief so potent it almost knocked him from his saddle.

But their respite was short-lived. The sight of the outlaws spurred them onward, and the relentless pace resumed. The plains stretched before them, offering a vast expanse of open space but also providing little cover. The outlaws, despite their lagging pursuit, had the advantage of the open terrain.

As dusk approached, casting long shadows across the landscape, they encountered a small cluster of gnarled, ancient trees offering a temporary refuge. They dismounted, their legs unsteady from the relentless chase. The horses, equally exhausted, needed a moment to recover.

Man From Tennessee

They checked their wounds. Elias discovered a grazing wound on his arm, a testament to the near misses during their escape. Kiowa, surprisingly, seemed unscathed, his movements still fluid and graceful, although exhaustion etched itself on his features.

With the darkness descending, they decided to rest and prepare for the night. Finding a relatively sheltered spot under the protective canopy of the trees, they settled down for the night, wary of any lingering danger. They ate some of their meager rations, their stomachs full of the gnawing anxiety of their near-death experience.

As the moon cast its ethereal glow upon the landscape, the stark reality of their situation weighed heavily upon them. They had escaped, for now, but the danger wasn't over. The outlaws might regroup, and the vastness of the plains offered little protection against their relentless pursuit. They needed to make plans. They needed to escape again.

Elias, his mind racing, began to formulate a strategy. They would have to make their way to a larger settlement, a place where they would find safety in numbers. He knew that they couldn't rely solely on their physical capabilities; their luck was running low.

A Narrow Escape

Under the watchful eye of the moon, they planned their escape. They would avoid the main trails, taking less traveled paths and relying on Kiowa's intimate knowledge of the area to avoid detection. They would travel during the night, using the cover of darkness to their advantage, emerging into the day only when necessary. They would stay vigilant, their senses constantly alert and always ready for another confrontation.

The coming days would be a continuation of their desperate flight. But tonight, under the quiet blanket of night, they rested, the quiet peace of the desert night temporarily calming their racing hearts. Their escape had been a narrow one, but they had lived to fight another day. The mountains had tested their limits, and they had endured. But their journey was far from over. The road ahead remained long and perilous, but for now, they had found a fleeting respite. Their survival was a testament to their resilience, their skill, and their unbreakable bond. They had escaped the mountains and the mayhem they contained, but the wilderness still held its secrets, and the threat of the outlaws still loomed. Their journey for freedom was still far from complete.

Chapter 14

Betrayal and Trust

The next morning dawned gray and cold, a stark contrast to the fiery sunset that had marked their harrowing escape. The meager breakfast of hardtack and jerky did little to alleviate the gnawing hunger in their bellies, a hunger mirrored by the unspoken tension that hung heavy between Elias and Kiowa. The previous day's events had forged a fragile bond of survival, but beneath the surface, a deep chasm of mistrust was beginning to form.

Elias, his arm throbbing with a dull ache, eyed Kiowa with a mixture of suspicion and apprehension. Kiowa, seemingly unfazed by their precarious situation, meticulously cleaned and oiled his rifle, his movements precise and economical. The silence between them was thick with unspoken accusations, each man harboring doubts about the other's true motives.

"We need to reach Harmony Creek," Elias finally said, his voice rough from lack of sleep and the strain of their flight. "It's the closest settlement, and we'll find help there."

Man From Tennessee

Kiowa looked up, his dark eyes unwavering. "Harmony Creek is a long way," he replied, his tone measured. "And the path is fraught with danger. There are other, safer routes we could take."

Elias's brow furrowed. "Safer? What safer routes? You haven't mentioned any others. Why are you being so evasive?"

Kiowa rose slowly, his movements suggesting a coiled spring ready to unleash its pent-up energy. "I am choosing the safest path for us," he replied, his voice low but firm.

"You trust my judgment when it comes to navigating these mountains. Why do you doubt it now?" "Because you haven't told me where we're going!" Elias retorted, his voice rising. "You've been leading us in circles since we escaped the outlaws. Where are you really taking me?"

The accusation hung in the air, thick and heavy, threatening to shatter the fragile truce that had held them together. Kiowa's hand instinctively went to the butt of his rifle, his eyes narrowing. The sudden movement sent a shiver down Elias's spine.

"I am taking you to safety," Kiowa said, his voice strained. "But safety isn't always where you think it is. Sometimes, the most dangerous paths lead to the safest destinations."

Betrayal and Trust

"I don't believe you," Elias countered. "You're hiding something from me. What is it, Kiowa? Why are you really leading me away from Harmony Creek?"

Kiowa's eyes flickered, a brief moment of vulnerability crossing his face before a hardened expression quickly masked it. "There are those who would seek to harm you in Harmony Creek, those who would not hesitate to finish what the outlaws started," he replied, his voice barely a whisper. "I know things you don't. I have reasons you wouldn't understand."

The words hung between them, a dense fog of suspicion and half-truths. Elias felt a knot tightening in his stomach. He had placed his trust in this man and risked his life on his expertise, and now, he felt the cold hand of betrayal. He was not sure whether he should believe him or not. Each word felt like a calculated step in a deadly game of cat and mouse. He sensed Kiowa's reticence wasn't just about the dangers of Harmony Creek; there was something more.

The ensuing silence stretched into an uncomfortable eternity, punctuated only by the chirping of unseen birds and the rustling of leaves. The air crackled with the unspoken tension, a silent battle of wills waged between two men bound together by circumstance and separated by mistrust.

Man From Tennessee

Elias knew he had to proceed carefully. Accusations would only solidify the wall of silence between them. He needed to find a way to break through Kiowa's defenses and uncover the truth behind his evasiveness.

"Let's assume, for the sake of argument, that you are right," Elias said, choosing his words carefully. "That Harmony Creek is not safe. Then what is your plan? Where are you taking me?"

Kiowa hesitated, his eyes darting around as if searching for an answer that he couldn't quite find. Finally, he spoke, his voice low and gravelly. "There is a hidden valley, far from the main trails, a place where even the most ruthless outlaws wouldn't dare venture. It's a perilous journey, but it is a secure route. It's the only place where you will be safe."

"And what about the outlaws?" Elias asked, his suspicion lingering. "They'll still be searching for me. How do we avoid them?"

"We will use the shadows, the cover of night, and the secret paths known only to those who live in this land. We will avoid settlements and hide in the mountains, waiting until the heat dies down. Then, we will emerge. It is the only way to ensure your survival, Elias."

Betrayal and Trust

Elias pondered this. Kiowa's argument held some weight. He could admit he was not a master strategist, nor was he intimately familiar with the rugged terrain. Kiowa's knowledge could be vital. Yet, a sliver of doubt remained. Was this truly the path to safety, or was it a path designed to lead him into even greater danger?

Trust had been broken, but the alternative was to continue onward alone, with a stranger's rifle aimed squarely at his back. Elias was left with a difficult decision. He was certain that there was more to Kiowa's story than what he was revealing, but trusting Kiowa was the only option that seemed to present a viable escape from the shadow of his pursuers. His escape was no longer just about eluding his enemies but also about deciphering the cryptic intentions of his guide.

They continued their journey, a silent pact forged between them, a precarious alliance built on necessity and a shared desire to survive. But beneath the surface, the simmering mistrust remained, a constant undercurrent threatening to derail their precarious journey toward an uncertain future. The mountains were silent witnesses to their unspoken conflict, their jagged peaks mirroring the jagged edges of their fragile alliance. Each step forward was a step further into the unknown, a gamble on the trustworthiness of a man whose motives were as shrouded in mystery as the mountains themselves. Elias's fate rested not only on his own cunning and survival skills but also on a fragile thread of trust—a thread that could snap at any moment. As the sun dipped below the horizon, painting the sky in hues of blood orange and deep violet, Elias knew that their journey was far from over, and the true test of their uneasy alliance was yet to come. The mountains, silent sentinels, held their breath, waiting to see who would triumph in this silent battle of wills—a dance between betrayal and trust, played out against the harsh backdrop of the unforgiving wilderness.

Chapter 15
A Glimmer of Hope

The wind, a biting, relentless force, whipped at Elias's coat as he crested the final ridge. His breath plumed white in the frigid air, a stark contrast to the sweat beading on his forehead. Days blurred into a relentless cycle of climbing, descending, and hiding, each sunrise bringing a fresh wave of exhaustion and a renewed sense of dread. Kiowa, his taciturn guide, remained silent, his gaze fixed on the trail ahead, his face as impassive as the granite peaks surrounding them. The unspoken tension between them, a constant undercurrent throughout their journey—remained, a fragile truce held together by necessity alone.

The physical toll of the journey was immense. Elias's arm, still throbbing from the outlaw's bullet, ached with every movement. His boots were worn through, his clothes ragged and torn, his body weary beyond measure. Hunger gnawed at his stomach, a constant companion that only intensified the gnawing fear. He had lost track of time—of days, of hope. He had surrendered to the rhythm of the mountains, a relentless cycle of exertion and survival, where each breath was a victory, each step forward a testament to his will.

Yet, amidst the despair and physical suffering, a flicker of hope had begun to ignite—a small ember against the overwhelming darkness. It wasn't a sudden revelation, a miraculous sign, but a gradual dawning, a subtle shift in perception that sparked a new determination to continue. The flicker started with small things: the sight of a deer grazing peacefully in a hidden meadow, the unexpected warmth of the midday sun breaking through the clouds, the simple comfort of sharing a meager meal with Kiowa, a silent acknowledgment of their shared plight. These small moments of grace, interwoven with the harsh realities of their escape, had gradually chipped away at the despair.

Then, it happened.

As they rounded a bend, a small, weathered cabin came into view, nestled amidst a cluster of pines. Smoke curled lazily from its chimney, a comforting plume against the stark, gray sky. Elias's heart quickened. He recognized the design—the distinctive angle of the roof, the small porch that sagged slightly under the weight of time and weather. It was his sister's cabin, a haven he had only dreamed of reaching.

A Glimmer of Hope

A wave of emotion, so intense it almost overwhelmed him, washed over Elias—relief, joy, gratitude—a complex cocktail of feelings that left him breathless. He had never felt so profoundly grateful for something so simple, so tangible: the sight of a familiar structure in a vast, unforgiving wilderness. It wasn't just a place of shelter; it represented safety, family, the possibility of healing, and respite. The years spent wandering the plains as a rancher, the hardships endured after he left his family's farm to forge his own path, seemed to melt away in the face of this unexpected sight.

He urged Kiowa onward, his voice hoarse with emotion. Kiowa, ever watchful, had spotted it at the same moment. His usually stoic features softened slightly, a hint of something akin to relief—or perhaps even something he had previously dismissed as sentimentality—passing across his face. They moved with renewed vigor, their steps lighter, and their pace quicker. The climb to the cabin was the hardest yet; it tested everything Elias had left in him, but he pushed onward, fueled by the tantalizing prospect of safety and the hope of seeing his sister's face once again.

The cabin stood at the edge of a small, sheltered valley, a sanctuary carved from the harsh embrace of the mountains. The pines provided a natural barrier, shielding it from the wind and the cold. A small stream gurgled nearby, its gentle murmur a soothing counterpoint to the roar of the wind high above. The contrast between the untamed wilderness and the relative tranquility of the valley was stark and striking—a visual representation of Elias's own journey from despair to hope.

As they approached, a figure emerged from the cabin. A woman, her hair streaked with gray, her face etched with the marks of time and hardship, stood on the porch, her eyes wide with surprise and then recognition. It was Sarah, Elias's sister, her appearance unchanged from their last meeting. His breath hitched in his throat; he could barely speak. The sight of his sister, her face etched with worry, made the journey worth it. He had made it home.

Sarah rushed toward him, her arms open. Their embrace was long and silent, a torrent of unspoken words exchanged in a single, profound moment. Tears streamed down Elias's face, a mixture of relief, gratitude, and the accumulated emotional weight of his arduous escape. This was more than just finding shelter; this was a return to something he had almost given up on. The safety he had craved, the haven from the unrelenting danger, was here, in the arms of his loved one.

A Glimmer of Hope

In the warmth of the cabin, with a mug of steaming broth in his hands, Elias felt a sense of peace he hadn't experienced in months. The fire crackled merrily, casting dancing shadows on the walls, a comforting counterpoint to the turmoil still brewing within him. Kiowa sat quietly in a corner, observing them with a guarded curiosity. His silence, however, no longer felt accusatory; it held a quiet respect, a recognition of the emotional intensity of the reunion.

The respite, however, was temporary. The comfort of the cabin couldn't completely erase the threat that still loomed. The outlaws, driven by greed and vengeance, were still searching. The news of Elias's escape might reach them at any moment. The quiet valley could soon become a battleground. The sense of relief was temporary, for even the most peaceful valleys are not immune to the winds of chaos. The final confrontation was inevitable, a dark cloud hanging on the horizon. The sense of security, however genuine, was tinged with a lingering apprehension, a reminder that their journey was far from over. The mountains, silent witnesses to their escape, continued to watch, their imposing presence a constant reminder of the fragility of safety in a world of violence and treachery. He knew that he had a score to settle, a debt to repay. But for now, the warmth of his sister's embrace and the crackle of the fire provided the strength he needed to face the next challenge. He still bore the burden of his pursuer's wrath, however, a cloud that would soon reappear, casting a shadow over his moment of hope. And in the shadows, a darker threat, one that Kiowa had only begun to unveil—lurked in the background.

Chapter 16
Reunion and Relief

Sarah's embrace was a lifeline, a tangible connection to a life he'd almost lost. The scent of woodsmoke and pine needles mingled with the familiar fragrance of her lavender soap, a comforting aroma that transported him back to a time before the relentless pursuit, before the betrayals, before the bullet that still throbbed a dull ache in his arm. He buried his face in her hair, letting the tears flow freely—a release of the pent-up tension that had gripped him for weeks. He didn't speak, couldn't speak; the emotion was too raw, too overwhelming for words.

Sarah, her own eyes glistening with unshed tears, held him close, her touch grounding him in the present, anchoring him to a reality far removed from the desolate landscape they had just traversed. The cabin, small and simple, was a haven—a sanctuary against the harshness of the world outside. It smelled of woodsmoke, dried herbs, and the comforting warmth of a well-loved home. The rough-hewn furniture, worn but sturdy, spoke of a life lived simply, honestly, a life he had craved amidst the dangers he faced.

After a long, silent moment, Sarah gently pulled back, her gaze searching his face with a mixture of concern and relief. "Elias," she whispered, her voice thick with emotion, "you're safe." The simple statement held the weight of worlds, a reassurance that reverberated through him, calming the storm within. She examined his injuries, her touch gentle yet firm, her eyes filled with fierce protectiveness. The bullet wound, still raw and tender, elicited a wince from him, but the comforting presence of his sister overshadowed the pain.

"How...how did you know I'd come here?" he managed to ask, his voice hoarse from disuse and emotion.

Sarah smiled faintly, a bittersweet expression that spoke of hardships endured and sacrifices made. "I've been expecting you," she replied, her gaze drifting to the fire crackling merrily in the hearth. "Kiowa sent word a few days ago, a message carried by a trustworthy hand. He said you'd need a safe haven." She hesitated, then added, "He also said you'd be in trouble."

Elias exchanged a glance with Kiowa, who sat quietly in a corner, his usual impassivity replaced with a cautious watchfulness. The unspoken communication between them was a silent acknowledgment of the gravity of their situation. Their reunion, however joyous, was merely a temporary reprieve. The threat still loomed, a shadow clinging to the edges of their newfound safety.

It was Sarah who broke the silence, a concerned frown etching itself onto her face. "It's not just the outlaws, Elias," she said, her voice low and grave. "There's something else. Something bigger."

She proceeded to recount a tale of hushed whispers in the nearby town, of shadowy figures seen lurking in the mountains, and of a conspiracy woven into the very fabric of their peaceful valley. It was a story of land grabs, of powerful men manipulating events from the shadows, of a hidden agenda far more sinister than a mere band of outlaws seeking revenge. She spoke of a clandestine meeting witnessed by a terrified townsman—a meeting in which names were mentioned, names that sent a chill down Elias's spine—names connected to powerful men in far-off cities, men who held sway over land and law, men who considered themselves above it all.

The revelation sent a jolt of icy dread through Elias. It was more than just the outlaws pursuing him for a past act of defiance; it was a well-organized, far-reaching scheme. The pursuit was not personal, not merely about vengeance—it was a calculated move in a larger game, a game that threatened not only his life but the lives of everyone in the valley. The outlaws were merely pawns, expendable pieces in a much larger, more dangerous contest.

Sarah described a pattern of intimidation, of land deeds mysteriously disappearing and families being forced off their land. The town, once a haven of quiet stability, was now living under the shadow of fear. The outlaws, though dangerous, were a threat they could perhaps handle. This new revelation was far more frightening—an unseen force, powerful and merciless, pulling the strings from a distance.

The news, while shattering the brief peace of their reunion, invigorated Elias. The comforting warmth of the cabin seemed to diminish against the looming threat. It was a chilling narrative that twisted the simple pursuit into a complex, web-like conspiracy. The outlaws were suddenly inconsequential, mere players in a much larger, more intricate game that played out in the shadows of the valley. This new reality brought a sobering weight of responsibility. His fight was not just about survival; it was about protecting his sister and the valley residents and confronting a power far greater than he could have ever imagined.

He felt a renewed sense of purpose, a grim determination hardening his resolve. The danger was amplified, magnified beyond his initial fears. His personal vendetta against the outlaws suddenly became secondary to a larger struggle against an unseen enemy. He had faced the harsh realities of the mountains and now faced an even steeper challenge: facing powerful forces that threatened everything he held dear.

The next few hours were spent in earnest conversation—a grim council of war between Sarah and Elias, with Kiowa observing from the corner, his silent presence a palpable presence amidst the seriousness of their situation. They analyzed the information Sarah had gathered, piecing together the fragmented clues, and searching for a way to understand the extent of the conspiracy. The small cabin, once a haven of peace, transformed into a strategic command center, the firelight illuminating their determined faces as they plotted their next course of action.

The quiet murmur of voices, the rustling of papers, and the occasional sharp intake of breath filled the cabin. They needed to find a way to unravel the conspiracy, to expose those pulling the strings, to protect the innocent. This task was now Elias's responsibility. He had to use his wits, his strength, and the strength of his family to combat the new threat that reached beyond the mountains and valleys.

As the night deepened, exhaustion finally weighed down Elias. Yet, the weight of the day's revelations lingered. He found comfort in Sarah's arms, but still, the shadows danced in his mind. He looked at his sister with a newfound determination. The relief of reunion was still present, but it was now overshadowed by the dark realization of the larger conflict ahead. This was no longer simply a personal fight for survival. This fight was for everything they held dear—for the valley, for the people, and for the future that lay ahead, shrouded in both danger and uncertainty. The threat was larger than he ever could have imagined. The mountains themselves seemed to hold their breath, anticipating the coming storm.

The next morning, they developed a plan—a risky, almost desperate gamble, but one they had to take. The fight would now be against a formidable and hidden enemy, a fight where the stakes were higher than ever. The reunion had been a moment of respite, a brief taste of normalcy in a turbulent world. But the respite was short-lived. The fight was far from over. The shadows lurking in the corners of the valley, the whispered secrets, the hidden agendas—they were now Elias's

Reunion and Relief

new enemy, and he would face them with the same tenacity and courage that had carried him through his perilous escape. The valley, once a sanctuary, now stood on the brink of a storm—a storm that only Elias could hope to weather.

Chapter 17
Unraveling the Mystery

The crisp morning air bit at Elias's cheeks, a stark contrast to the warmth of the cabin fire that had kept them company through the long night. He watched Sarah as she meticulously packed a small knapsack, her movements precise and efficient, a stark contrast to the anxiety that flickered in her eyes. She was a woman of action, a force of nature disguised in the gentle grace of a woman who had known hardship but refused to be broken by it.

"Ready?" he asked, his voice raspy from lack of sleep but firm with resolve.

Sarah nodded, her gaze meeting his. "As I'll ever be. Kiowa's already scouted the path to Widow McGregor's place. She's the only one who might know something about the missing land deeds."

Widow McGregor, a woman as weathered and resilient as the mountain pines themselves, lived on the outskirts of town, a recluse who had fiercely guarded her property against the creeping encroachment of progress. Rumors whispered of hidden tunnels beneath her ramshackle house, relics of a time long past—a time of secrets and buried treasures.

The journey to Widow McGregor's was fraught with the quiet tension that had become their constant companion. The beauty of the valley, normally a source of peace, now seemed to hold its breath, the silence punctuated only by the crunch of leaves under their boots and the occasional rustle in the undergrowth. Kiowa, ever vigilant, trailed behind them, his presence a silent reassurance.

Widow McGregor's house was a testament to time's relentless march. The wood was grey with age, the windows clouded with dust, and the roof sagged under the weight of years. But despite its dilapidated state, there was an air of defiance about it, a stubborn refusal to yield to decay.

The old woman greeted them with a suspicious squint. Her eyes, though clouded with age, held a sharp intelligence that belied her appearance. Sarah, with her gentle demeanor and quiet confidence, managed to ease the old woman's initial wariness. She spoke of shared concerns, of a common enemy threatening their peaceful valley, and slowly, tentatively, Widow McGregor opened up.

Unraveling the Mystery

She spoke in hushed tones, her voice raspy and thin but filled with a fierce determination. She confirmed the rumors of the land grab, detailing how seemingly reputable men—local power brokers—had strong-armed families into signing over their land for a pittance. She spoke of hushed meetings, threats, and intimidation, her words painting a picture of a conspiracy far more sinister than Elias had initially imagined.

"They're after the old mines," she rasped, her voice barely a whisper. "The ones nobody's touched in decades. They say there's something valuable hidden deep inside, something worth more than all the land in the valley."

Elias's heart pounded. The old mines—legends whispered of hidden riches within their depths—riches that had lured prospectors to their doom for generations. But this wasn't about gold or silver; it was about something far more valuable, something that could fuel this insidious conspiracy.

As they delved deeper into the conversation, a name emerged—Bartholomew Thorne. A wealthy landowner and a respected member of the community, Thorne was the linchpin of this conspiracy. He was the one pulling the strings, using the outlaws as his muscle, manipulating the legal system to his advantage. The missing land deeds were just a part of a larger scheme to acquire control of the old mines.

Man From Tennessee

Widow McGregor produced a weathered ledger, its pages brittle with age but filled with meticulous records. It contained detailed information on land ownership, property transactions, and a series of coded entries that hinted at Thorne's activities. It was a risky gamble to trust this information to this woman, but the desperation of the situation compelled them to give her a chance. The risk was significant.

Sarah's sharp eye caught a peculiar pattern in the coded entries—a series of symbols that resembled the markings on an old map she'd seen once in her father's belongings. The map was rumored to lead to a hidden chamber within the mines. It was a tantalizing clue, a potential pathway to unraveling the entire conspiracy.

Leaving Widow McGregor's house, the three rode in a somber mood. They now possessed a tangible piece of evidence—a roadmap leading them to the heart of the conspiracy. As they rode into the twilight, the mountains silhouetted against the setting sun, the weight of their discovery heavy on their shoulders. They weren't just fighting outlaws anymore; they were fighting a powerful, well-entrenched enemy with the support of many local officials.

That evening, huddled around the fire, they studied the ledger and the map, deciphering the coded entries and piecing together the puzzle. The map indicated a hidden entrance to the mines concealed behind a waterfall on the far side of the valley. The ledger detailed Thorne's associates—a network of corrupt officials and land speculators complicit in his scheme.

As the night wore on, the pieces of the puzzle began to fall into place. They discovered that Thorne's scheme extended far beyond land grabs. He intended to use the mines to extract some powerful substance—some mineral or artifact—that was far more valuable than any gold or silver. The exact nature of this material was still a mystery, but it was clear that the conspiracy extended deep into powerful circles.

Their investigations unearthed evidence of intimidation, threats, and even violence against those who dared stand in Thorne's way. The outlaws were just the beginning. This went deeper. Much deeper.

The revelation of Thorne's complicity sent a chill down Elias's spine. This wasn't just a local land grab; it was a meticulously planned operation with far-reaching consequences. The implications extended beyond the valley, threatening to destabilize the entire region. It was a significant escalation, far more threatening than anything they had ever encountered. The weight of responsibility settled heavily on

Elias's shoulders; he was no longer just fighting for his own survival. He was fighting for the soul of the valley.

Their plan, forged in the firelight of the small cabin, was a dangerous one. They would infiltrate Thorne's operation, expose his scheme, and bring him to justice. It was a high-stakes gamble, one that could cost them everything. But they had no choice. The quiet desperation that had gripped the valley had finally turned into a fiery determination to fight back.

The next morning dawned clear and cold, the rising sun painting the mountain peaks with a breathtaking palette of gold and rose. But beneath the surface of beauty, the threat of the conspiracy still loomed, a dark cloud threatening to engulf everything they held dear. The journey ahead was perilous, and the stakes were higher than ever. But Elias, Sarah, and Kiowa stood ready to face whatever lay ahead, united in their determination to unravel the mystery of Thorne's scheme and protect their valley from the encroaching darkness. The fight had just begun

Chapter 18

Facing the Conspiracy

The dusty air of the Golden Spur Saloon hung thick with the smell of stale whiskey and sweat. The flickering gas lamps cast long, dancing shadows across the rough-hewn tables, illuminating the faces of the men gathered inside. Elias sat alone, nursing a lukewarm glass of beer, his gaze sweeping across the room, assessing the players in this deadly game. He'd chosen this place—the heart of Thorne's influence, for their meeting; a gamble, yes, but a necessary one.

Bartholomew Thorne, a man whose reputation preceded him like a thunderclap, arrived late. He was impeccably dressed, his expensive suit a stark contrast to the rough and tumble atmosphere of the saloon. Two hulking men flanked him, their hands resting casually near their holsters, a silent threat hanging in the air. Thorne's smile didn't reach his eyes; it was a thin, predatory expression that sent a shiver down Elias's spine.

Man From Tennessee

"Mr. Cole," Thorne's voice was smooth, cultured, a deceptive veneer over the steel beneath. "I must say, I'm surprised you dared to accept my invitation."

Elias met Thorne's gaze without flinching. "I'm a man of my word, Mr. Thorne. And I'm curious. Curious about your... ambitions concerning the old mines."

Thorne chuckled, a low, rumbling sound. "Ambitions? A strong word, wouldn't you agree? I merely intend to develop some underutilized resources. For the good of the community, of course."

"Underutilized resources that you intend to acquire by any means necessary," Elias countered, his voice calm but firm. He produced Widow McGregor's ledger, laying it on the table. "This suggests otherwise. It details your... less-than-legal methods of acquiring land."

Thorne's smile vanished. He picked up the ledger, his fingers tracing the brittle pages. He glanced at the coded entries, a flicker of surprise in his eyes. "Interesting. I'd be inclined to think this... 'Evidence' is a fabrication."

"I assure you, it's not," Elias said, his gaze unwavering. He reached into his coat and produced Sarah's map. "This, however, is something you might find more difficult to dismiss.

Facing the Conspiracy

It shows a hidden entrance to the mines—an entrance you and
your associates have conveniently 'overlooked' in your land
surveys."

The tension in the room tightened, palpable and
suffocating. Thorne's two bodyguards shifted their weight,
their eyes fixed on Elias, a silent warning. Thorne, however,
remained outwardly calm, his mask of composure undisturbed.

"Let's not play games, Mr. Cole," Thorne said, his voice
losing its veneer of civility. "What do you want?"

"I want you to stop," Elias stated simply. "Leave the mines
alone. Leave the valley alone."

Thorne laughed, a harsh, bitter sound. "And if I refuse?"

"Then we'll make sure everyone knows about your...
'underutilized resources,'" Elias retorted, his hand resting
casually near the gun concealed beneath his coat. "About the
intimidation, the threats, the violence. We have enough
evidence to hang you and your entire operation."

A long silence followed, broken only by the muted clinking
of glasses from the other patrons of the saloon. Thorne studied
Elias, his gaze searching, assessing.

"You're bluffing," Thorne said finally, his voice low and dangerous. "You have nothing concrete. Just hearsay and a curious map."

"Perhaps," Elias conceded, his voice laced with a subtle threat. "But I have something you don't—Sarah's testimony. And the backing of people who are tired of your intimidation and corruption. People who are ready to fight back. We can take this to the authorities, even if it means involving the territory's governor, who isn't as corrupt as some might assume."

Thorne considered this, his face a mask of controlled fury. He knew Elias was telling the truth. The evidence might be circumstantial, but the threat was real. He'd underestimated this seemingly simple rancher.

"This doesn't have to end violently," Thorne said, his voice regaining a semblance of control. "We can reach a compromise."

"What kind of compromise?" Elias asked, his eyes narrowed.

"I'll withdraw from the mines," Thorne offered, "in exchange for discretion. Let's say, a sizable sum to ensure your silence."

Facing the Conspiracy

Elias knew Thorne was trying to buy him off, but it was a calculated risk. He was close to winning. He had to be cautious. He couldn't afford to let Thorne manipulate the situation anymore.

"That's not enough," Elias countered, buying himself time. "I need assurances that you'll stop your land grabs completely. Full restitution to those you've wronged. And a guarantee that your associates will face the music."

Thorne's jaw clenched. This was more than he'd anticipated. He was losing control. But the thought of exposure, of his carefully constructed empire crumbling, pushed him further into this deal.

"Very well," Thorne conceded, his voice tight with barely contained rage. "I'll agree to your terms. But this ends here. Consider it a costly lesson learned, Mr. Cole."

Elias nodded. He knew this was a temporary victory. Thorne was a dangerous man, and he'd be back. But for now, he'd secured a crucial win. Leaving the saloon, the weight of the valley's future no longer felt entirely crushing. He had bought them valuable time to find evidence to prove Thorne's wrongdoings and bring him to justice for good. The fight was far from over, but the path forward was at least a little clearer.

Man From Tennessee

The confrontation had been tense, a dangerous game of wits, but Elias had emerged victorious, his courage and intelligence proving to be a formidable weapon. As he rode away, the rising sun casting long shadows behind him, the sound of Thorne's defeated muttering seemed to echo in the air, a testament to Elias's triumph.

Chapter 19
Unexpected Allies

The agreement with Thorne felt like a fragile truce, a temporary reprieve in a war far from over. Elias knew he couldn't rest on his laurels. Thorne's word was as flimsy as a desert bloom; he needed more than a promise and irrefutable proof. And to gather that proof, he needed help. He rode toward Widow McGregor's farm, the setting sun painting the sky in hues of orange and purple, a deceptive beauty masking the darkness that still clung to the valley.

Widow McGregor, a woman etched with the hardships of life on the frontier, greeted him with a weary but knowing smile. Though lined with age, her eyes held a spark of defiance that mirrored his own. The ledger he'd shown Thorne had been only a fragment of her meticulous records, a testament to years of observing Thorne's corrupt dealings.

"They're afraid, Elias," she whispered, her voice raspy from years of whispering secrets. "Afraid of Thorne and his men. But they're not all silent."

114

Man From Tennessee

She led him to a hidden meeting place, a small, forgotten grove nestled amongst the towering pines that shielded it from prying eyes. There, huddled around a crackling fire, sat a handful of men and women—farmers, ranchers, shopkeepers—the silent victims of Thorne's tyranny. Their faces, etched with suspicion and fear, bore witness to the pervasive shadow of Thorne's power.

Elias, a stranger until that moment, spoke not of grand pronouncements or heroic gestures but of shared grievances and common fears. He spoke of the land grabs, the threats, and the subtle coercion that had slowly strangled the life from their community. He showed them Sarah's map, not as a weapon but as a symbol of hope, a testament to the courage of a woman who dared to challenge the seemingly invincible.

His words resonated with them. They were not foolish people; they knew the risks and the potential consequences. But years of silent suffering had bred a quiet desperation, a yearning for justice that outweighed their fear. Their silence, they realized, had emboldened Thorne. Their silence had allowed him to fester and thrive.

One by one, they shared their stories. Old Man Fitzwilliam, whose farm had been mysteriously "bought" for a pittance, his voice trembling with indignation. Martha Jenkins, whose husband had mysteriously disappeared after confronting Thorne's men, her eyes filled with silent grief. And then there was Silas, the blacksmith, a man whose hands were more accustomed to shaping metal than holding a weapon but whose eyes burned with righteous anger.

These were not hardened outlaws or seasoned revolutionaries; they were ordinary people, ordinary victims of an extraordinary evil. But in their quiet desperation, Elias saw a strength, a resolve, a unity that surprised even him. It wasn't a call to arms but a quiet acknowledgment of a shared fate, a shared enemy... a shared desire for a better future.

They began to unravel the web of Thorne's lies, piecing together fragments of information, shared observations, and suppressed memories. They spoke of the coded messages they'd glimpsed in Thorne's correspondence, the unusual activity around the old mines, and the disappearances that were conveniently swept under the rug by local authorities.

Silas, the blacksmith, revealed he'd managed to secretly duplicate some key documents—contracts, land deeds, even letters detailing Thorne's bribery of local officials—forged through weeks of nervous nights working under the cloak of darkness. The documents weren't easy to handle, but they were strong enough to stand as evidence of Thorne's corrupt dealings. It was a dangerous undertaking, but his quiet act of defiance was a pivotal moment in their rebellion.

Over several nights, Elias helped them analyze the documents, cross-referencing the information with Widow McGregor's ledger. The truth, hidden beneath layers of deceit, began to emerge. Thorne's empire, it turned out, was built on a foundation of lies and intimidation. His "community development" was a thinly veiled cover for land grabbing, extortion, and resource exploitation.

As the puzzle pieces fell into place, a new strength emerged from their shared vulnerability. They were no longer isolated individuals, each facing Thorne's wrath alone. They were a coalition, a collective force bound by a shared purpose and fueled by a fit of collective anger. Their unity became their greatest weapon, a force far more powerful than anyone could have mustered alone.

Their clandestine meetings continued under the shroud of night, a testament to the courage of ordinary individuals rising against a seemingly insurmountable foe. The grove became a sanctuary, a place where fear gave way to hope, whispers became plans, and isolated grievances coalesced into a collective roar of defiance.

Unexpected Allies

Initially a stranger, Elias became their leader, not through coercion or authority, but through respect. He brought a sense of structure to their haphazard rebellion, guiding them with his knowledge of Thorne's methods and his understanding of the legal system, however flawed it was in that corrupt territory. He taught them how to gather evidence, document their accounts, and prepare for the inevitable confrontation.

The women, initially hesitant, began to play crucial roles. Martha Jenkins, though still grieving her husband's disappearance, became a vital source of information, remembering details that others had overlooked. Other women in the community shared their experiences, adding crucial insights and observations. It wasn't a romantic revolution but a practical, determined uprising born of necessity and fueled by a shared desire for justice.

The meetings weren't solely focused on strategy. There were moments of shared grief, quiet tears, and unspoken fears.

But the undercurrent of their discussions always circled back to the need for action, change, and reclaim their lives and their valley from Thorne's grasp.

One evening, under the silent pines' watchful gaze, Elias realised his alliance's true significance. He wasn't just fighting for himself, Sarah, or even the valley; he was fighting for the essence of justice, for the power of ordinary people to rise up against oppression, challenge tyranny, and find hope in the most unexpected places.

The fight was far from over, but he no longer felt alone. He had found his army, not in the ranks of a well-trained militia, but in the hearts of ordinary people, finally finding their voices. And that, he realized, was a force far more powerful than any gun or gold mine. The coming confrontation would be dangerous, but it would be a fight fueled not by fear but by hope, by the unwavering belief in the power of unity and the unexpected strength of unlikely allies.

Chapter 20
Preparing for Confrontation

The air in the grove hung heavy with the scent of pine and anticipation. The crackling fire cast dancing shadows on the faces of Elias's unlikely army, etching their expressions in the flickering light. The previous nights had been spent piecing together Thorne's web of deceit, but this night was dedicated to dismantling it. Silence, once their refuge, now felt like a suffocating blanket. The quiet rustle of leaves, the distant hoot of an owl, each sound amplified the tension that hung in the air, thick and palpable.

Elias, no longer the stranger who had arrived only days before, stood at the heart of the group, a quiet authority radiating from him. He held Silas's meticulously copied documents—contracts, land deeds, letters—clutched tightly in his hand, tangible evidence of Thorne's crimes. The weight of the valley's fate rested on these fragile papers, on the shoulders of these ordinary people who had found extraordinary courage within themselves.

Man From Tennessee

"We've uncovered a rot that runs deep," Elias began, his voice low but firm, carrying over the crackling fire. "Thorne didn't just steal land; he stole livelihoods, hope, and, in some cases, lives. We have the proof. Now, we need a plan."

He unfolded Sarah's map, the faded ink starkly contrasting the intensity in his eyes. "This isn't just about land deeds and contracts; it's about reclaiming our valley, lives, and future. Thorne has fortified his position, but he's underestimated us. He's underestimated the power of a community united."

The map, a patchwork of trails, landmarks, and hidden routes, became the canvas for their strategy. They meticulously plotted Thorne's likely defenses, identifying weak points and potential escape routes. Despite his trembling hands, Old Man Fitzwilliam offered invaluable insight into the layout of Thorne's compound, a knowledge gleaned from years of observing Thorne's men's secretive comings and goings. Martha Jenkins, her grief momentarily overshadowed by a steely determination, recalled the locations of hidden supply caches, details she'd overheard in hushed conversations.

Silas, the blacksmith, surprisingly adept at strategy, suggested a diversionary tactic, using a small contingent to create a distraction while the main force approached Thorne's main house. He'd even crafted makeshift smoke bombs from readily available materials, a testament to his ingenuity and resourcefulness. The women, initially hesitant to participate in direct confrontation, volunteered to act as lookouts and messengers, utilizing their intimate knowledge of the valley's hidden paths and trails. Their sharp eyes and quiet efficiency would prove invaluable.

The hours drifted by, marked only by the shifting shadows and the quiet murmurs of strategic planning. They debated the optimal time for their attack—the cover of darkness or the chaotic confusion of dawn. The risks were discussed frankly, and the potential consequences were acknowledged without flinching. Death was a real possibility, a brutal reality they faced unflinchingly. Yet, fear was not the dominant emotion.

A strange mix of determination, anticipation, and a sense of shared purpose filled the grove.

As the night deepened, they dealt with the logistics—the distribution of weapons (mostly hunting rifles and shotguns, hastily cleaned and oiled), assigning roles, and planning escape routes in case of failure. The weapons were few, and the odds were stacked against them, but their unity was their greatest strength. They were no longer a collection of isolated victims but a force.

Man From Tennessee

Elias, throughout the planning, emphasized the importance of precision and speed. Their strength wasn't in brute force but in coordinated action and surprise. He stressed the need to overwhelm Thorne's men swiftly, to capture him before he could react or flee. He knew the authorities would likely be in Thorne's pocket, but the evidence they possessed was substantial.

Their preparations went beyond strategy and tactics. They shared stories, not just of Thorne's atrocities, but of their hopes and dreams for the future. They spoke of families, lost loved ones, and the simple joys they had been denied.

These weren't just battle plans being laid; it was a forging of bonds, a strengthening of resolve. The night wore on, the fire dying down to embers, mirroring the fading fear in their hearts. The quiet determination that settled over the group was both terrifying and inspiring.

They had faced a cruel master, a seemingly insurmountable foe, and instead of succumbing to despair, they had discovered strength in unity.

As the first streaks of dawn painted the eastern sky, Elias rose, a silhouette against the growing light. He held up Sarah's map, now creased and smudged but still a beacon of hope.

Preparing for Confrontation

"The dawn brings a reckoning," he stated, his voice ringing with conviction. "Tonight, we fight for our valley, our families, and our future. Tonight, we show Thorne and all those who would prey on the weak that silence no longer reigns."

A hush fell over the group, broken only by the chirping of birds welcoming the new day. They knew the risks. They knew the price of failure. But in their eyes, Elias saw not fear but an unwavering resolve, a quiet strength that could only be born from the depths of shared suffering and the heights of collective hope. The preparation was complete.

The confrontation was imminent. The fate of the valley hung in the balance, a balance now held precariously, yet firmly, in the hands of these ordinary people who had chosen to become extraordinary. The silence of the previous weeks was about to be shattered by a roar of defiance.

Chapter 21

The Final Confrontation

The sun beat down on Dust Devil Gulch, baking the wooden buildings and turning the dusty town square into an oven.

The air shimmered with heat, a cruel mirror reflecting the tension that hung heavy over the confrontation about to unfold. His face grim but determined, Elias positioned his small band of unlikely allies at strategic points around the square. They were outnumbered and outgunned, but their spirit, forged in the crucible of shared hardship and fueled by righteous fury, burned bright.

Thorne, perched on the balcony of the saloon—his makeshift headquarters—surveyed the scene with a chillingly calm demeanor. He was a man accustomed to power, to wielding fear as a weapon. But today, the fear seemed to be shifting, a subtle tremor in his usually unwavering gaze. He was surrounded by his men, rough-looking individuals, their faces hardened by years of intimidation and violence. They were loyal, for now, but the glint of unease in their eyes betrayed a hint of doubt.

The first shot shattered the oppressive silence. It came from Silas, positioned behind a weathered wagon, his aim true and his shot deadly. One of Thorne's men crumpled to the ground, the sharp crack of the rifle echoing through the square. This was the signal. Chaos erupted.

The firefight was brutal, a ballet of gunfire and desperate maneuvers. Martha Jenkins, her small frame surprisingly agile, weaved through the dust and smoke, her rifle spitting lead with deadly accuracy. Old Man Fitzwilliam, defying his age and frailty, provided covering fire from a recessed doorway, his shaky aim surprisingly effective. Even the women, armed with whatever they could find—hunting knives, rocks, even broken bottles—fought with a fierce determination that belied their gentle natures.

Elias, though, remained a calm eye in the storm. He moved with a practiced grace, his movements were precise and deadly.

His shots were deliberate, aimed not to kill but to disable, to incapacitate. He knew that their only hope lay in capturing

The Final Confrontation

Thorne alive, in preserving the evidence that would bring him down. He didn't want a bloodbath; he wanted justice.

The fight raged across the square, a cacophony of gunfire, shouts, and the sickening thud of bodies hitting the parched earth. Thorne's men, initially confident, began to falter. They were caught off guard, their expected easy victory dissolving into a desperate struggle for survival. Their discipline crumbled as Elias's forces pressed their advantage, their coordinated assault turning the tide.

Sarah, watching from a concealed position on the roof of a nearby building, adjusted her binoculars. Her heart pounded in her chest. She could see Elias, a relentless force amidst the chaos, working his way toward Thorne. She had played a crucial role in exposing Thorne's crimes, but seeing him fight face-to-face, she realized the real fight was here, in this dusty town square, under the unforgiving gaze of the desert sun.

As Thorne's men began to fall back, he retreated toward the saloon, his face contorted in a mixture of anger and fear. He had underestimated Elias and his allies. He had believed his power, his wealth, would protect him. He was wrong.

Elias, followed by a small group, burst through the saloon doors, finding Thorne cornered in his office. Thorne, his face pale, his usually arrogant demeanor replaced with a desperate plea, held a pistol to his head. He had a choice: fight to the death or surrender. The weight of his crimes, the magnitude of his lies, crushed him. He knew he had lost.

"It's over, Thorne," Elias said, his voice calm yet authoritative. "It's time to face the consequences of your actions."

Thorne, his eyes filled with the bitter knowledge of his defeat, lowered his weapon. He made a desperate attempt at defiance, but the fight had gone out of him.

The scene played out under the scorching sun. Dust motes danced in the air, illuminated by the setting sun, casting long shadows across the bloodstained square. Thorne's arrest was swift and orderly. The surviving members of his gang were rounded up, their resistance broken.

As the sun dipped below the horizon, painting the sky in hues of orange and purple, a sense of quiet relief settled over Dust Devil Gulch. The town square, scarred by battle, stood as a testament to the courage of those who had dared to challenge tyranny. The victory was hard-won, bought with sweat, blood, and unwavering resolve.

The Final Confrontation

Bruised but unbowed, Elias looked out at his allies, their faces reflecting a mixture of exhaustion and triumph. They had faced impossible odds and emerged victorious. They had reclaimed not just their land but their dignity, their hope.

The valley was theirs once more.

The arrests were made, and the evidence was secured, but the struggle had only just begun. The legal battles that followed were arduous and fraught with setbacks and delays.

With his vast resources, Thorne fought tooth and nail to evade justice. But Elias and his allies, armed with their evidence and supported by a community newly empowered, were relentless. They were no longer victims. They were warriors.

Their victory was not merely a military triumph but a victory for justice for the ordinary people who had dared to defy the powerful and the corrupt. Their fight resonated throughout the region. It inspired others to stand up against oppression and injustice. The story of Dust Devil Gulch became a legend, a reminder that even the most powerful can be brought down by the combined strength of a community united against tyranny. The silence of fear had been broken, replaced by the resounding echo of justice. And in the quiet aftermath of the battle, under the star-studded desert sky, Elias knew that the hard fight had been worth it. The valley and its people were finally free.

Chapter 22
A Desperate Fight for
Survival

The roar of gunfire was deafening. Dust, kicked up by the
frantic movement of men and horses, hung thick in the air,
obscuring vision and choking lungs. His eyes narrowed in
concentration, Elias moved like a phantom through the chaos,
his Colt Peacemaker a blur of motion. He wasn't aiming to kill;
his shots were precise and calculated to disarm, incapacitate,
and create openings for his allies. He knew that Thorne's men,
while brutal, were largely mercenaries motivated by greed, not
ideology. A few well-placed shots could shatter their morale
and turn the tide of the battle.

Martha Jenkins, a whirlwind of furious energy, fought with the
ferocity of a cornered badger. Her rifle barked relentlessly,
each shot finding its mark. She moved with surprising grace,
her small frame weaving through the storm of bullets and
flying debris. She'd learned to shoot as a girl, helping her father
protect their ranch from rustlers, and this experience served

her well. She was a force to be reckoned with, and the men who underestimated her paid the price.

Old Man Fitzwilliam, his face a mask of grim determination, continued to provide covering fire from his position. His aim was less precise than the others, but his shots were surprisingly effective, causing enough distraction to keep Thorne's men off balance. He fired with the measured precision of a lifetime spent hunting and defending his home. Each shot was a testament to his enduring grit and survival instinct. He symbolized the community's unwavering resistance, proving that age was no barrier to courage.

The women of Dust Devil Gulch, armed with whatever they could find—kitchen knives, rocks, even broken bottles—fought with a fierce determination that surprised even Elias. Their courage was born of desperation, of a desire to protect their homes, their families, their way of life. They formed a defensive wall, a human shield, their combined efforts slowing the advance of Thorne's men. Their screams were a battle cry, adding to the chaotic symphony of the conflict.

The battle raged across the square, a maelstrom of smoke, gunfire, and the sickening thud of falling bodies. The air was thick with the smell of gunpowder, sweat, and fear. Thorne's men, initially confident of victory, began to falter. Their discipline broke down, replaced by panic and desperation as they faced a far stronger and more determined resistance. Their ranks thinned, and casualties mounted with every passing minute.

From her vantage point on the roof, Sarah felt her heart pound in her chest. She'd meticulously documented Thorne's crimes, providing the evidence that had spurred Elias to action. But watching the battle unfold, she understood the true cost of justice. It wasn't just about legal documents and testimonies but bloodshed, sacrifice, and the unwavering courage of ordinary people fighting for their freedom.

Elias, seeing the turning tide, seized the opportunity. He led a small group of his most trusted allies in a coordinated assault on Thorne's remaining forces. They moved with a precision that spoke volumes of their training and experience, their movements fluid and deadly. They were a well-oiled machine, their actions perfectly synchronized, pushing back the enemy with unwavering determination.

Their movements were a symphony of coordinated attacks, decisively turning the tide of the battle.

The saloon, Thorne's makeshift headquarters, became the final battleground. The building groaned under the impact of gunfire, wood splintering, and glass shattering. Thorne's men, cornered and outnumbered, fought with the desperate fury of cornered animals. But Elias and his allies were relentless, pushing forward, inching closer to their ultimate goal.

The final confrontation took place in Thorne's office, a dimly lit room smelling of stale whiskey and cheap cigars. Thorne, his face pale and drawn, his eyes wide with terror, stood with his back against the wall, a pistol clutched in his trembling hand. The bravado, the arrogance that had characterized him for so long, had completely vanished. He was a broken man, his empire crumbling around him.

Elias faced him, his Colt Peacemaker trained but not yet raised. He didn't want to kill Thorne. He tried to bring him to justice. He wanted to make an example of him, to send a message to others who might consider following in his footsteps. "It's over, Thorne," Elias said, his voice steady and calm yet carrying the weight of authority. "It's time to face the consequences of your actions."

Thorne's eyes darted around the room, desperately searching for an escape, a way out of the situation he had created for himself. He saw none. The weight of his crimes, the magnitude of his deceit, was crushing him. He knew he had lost everything—his power, his wealth, his freedom. His defiant spirit was broken. He lowered his weapon with a shaky hand. His attempt at one last desperate act of defiance proved futile.

The sound of gunfire subsided, replaced by the ragged breaths of exhausted men and the quiet sobs of relieved women. The sun, dipping below the horizon, cast long shadows across the bloodstained square. The battle was over. Dust Devil Gulch had survived. Elias and his allies had prevailed. Their victory was a testament to their courage, determination, and unwavering belief in justice.

The arrests were swift and orderly. The surviving members of Thorne's gang were rounded up, their resistance broken. The weight of their defeat hung heavy upon them, their bravado replaced by the bitter taste of failure. Their dreams of wealth and power lay shattered in the dust.

A weary but triumphant silence settled over Dust Devil Gulch as darkness fell. Scarred by battle, the town square stood as a grim reminder of the price of freedom. But the scars were also marks of resilience, testaments to the indomitable spirit of a community that had refused to yield to oppression.

Bruised and exhausted, Elias stood amidst his allies, their faces mirroring his own mix of exhaustion and triumph.

Man From Tennessee

They had faced impossible odds, and against all expectations, they had prevailed. They had not only saved their homes and families but also their dignity and hope. The valley was theirs once more.

Their victory was not merely a military triumph; it was a victory for justice, a resounding affirmation of the power of ordinary people to stand up against tyranny. Their fight, their courage, became a beacon of hope, inspiring others to challenge oppression and injustice. The story of Dust Devil Gulch echoed throughout the West, a legend whispered around campfires and recounted in saloons—a reminder that even the most formidable foe could be defeated by the unwavering resolve of those who dared to fight for what was right. The legend of their victory served as a symbol of hope and resistance. Their fight became an inspiration to others, reminding them of the power of courage and unity.

Chapter 23
Justice Prevails

The air, still thick with the acrid smell of gunpowder, hung heavy and still. The sunset, a bruised purple bleeding into the darkening sky, cast long shadows across the ravaged town square. The silence, broken only by the occasional groan of a wounded man or the whimper of a frightened horse, was profoundly unsettling, a stark contrast to the cacophony of the battle that had just concluded. Elias, leaning against the weathered facade of the saloon, felt the tremors in his weary body. His muscles ached, his clothes were torn and stained, and a dull throbbing pulsed in his head. But the physical pain was nothing compared to the emotional weight that pressed down on him.

He surveyed the scene before him, a tableau of devastation and exhaustion. The square, once a bustling heart of Dust Devil Gulch, was now a battlefield strewn with broken wood, shattered glass, and the grim evidence of the battle. The bodies of Thorne's men lay scattered amidst the debris, a chilling testament to the violence that had erupted just hours before.

Man From Tennessee

The women of the town, their faces etched with exhaustion and relief, moved amongst the injured, tending to the wounds of their loved ones. Their resilience and unwavering courage in the face of such brutality filled him with a profound admiration.

Martha Jenkins, her rifle slung over her shoulder, approached him, her face smudged with grime and blood. A faint smile played on her lips, a testament to their shared victory. "We did it, Elias," she whispered, her voice hoarse. "We actually did it."

He nodded, unable to trust his own voice—the words caught in his throat, a mixture of relief and a profound sense of loss. The victory was hard-won, purchased with a price far steeper than he had ever anticipated. The faces of the fallen, both from his side and Thorne's, haunted his vision. He had sought justice, but the reality of achieving it left him feeling strangely empty.

Old Man Fitzwilliam, leaning heavily on his cane, hobbled toward them. His eyes, usually twinkling with mischievous humor, were clouded with weariness, but a spark of pride still flickered within their depths. He patted Elias on the shoulder, a gesture that spoke volumes of shared hardship and mutual respect. "You did good, son," he rasped, his voice strained but firm. "You did real good." His simple words held more weight than any grand declaration of victory.

The arrests, as swift and efficient as the final assault, had been chillingly final. Thorne, his arrogance replaced by a defeated and terrified humility, was led away in shackles.

The sight of his once-powerful figure, reduced to a cowering prisoner, was strangely anticlimactic. It wasn't the glorious, triumphant downfall he'd envisioned. The reality was far more complex, far more unsettling. The hollow victory lacked the satisfying catharsis he'd anticipated.

Elias found himself alone as darkness descended, his gaze fixed on the ravaged saloon, now silent and dark. The building stood as a skeletal reminder of the violence unleashed within its walls. The gunfire had ceased, but a sense of unease lingered. The echoes of the battle, both physical and emotional, reverberated through the night.

He thought of Sarah, her tireless work in gathering evidence against Thorne, the meticulous documentation that had laid the foundation for their actions. Her dedication and unflinching belief in justice were instrumental to their success. He knew that her contributions deserved recognition and that the fight for justice did not end with Thorne's capture. The deeper roots of corruption needed to be addressed.

The weight of responsibility settled upon his shoulders. This victory was only a single battle in a larger war against injustice and corruption. The fight for a truly just society was far from over, and the path ahead would be long and arduous. The wounds of Dust Devil Gulch, both physical and emotional, would take time to heal. He knew the true measure of their victory would be in their ability to rebuild, heal, and create a future where such violence would not be repeated.

The distant sound of weeping broke the quiet of the night. He followed the sound, finding a young woman, one of the townswomen who had fought so bravely alongside him, cradling the lifeless body of her husband. The raw grief etched upon her face struck him with a force that stripped away the remaining vestiges of triumph. The reality of the battle sunk in—the cost of justice, the loss, the sorrow. He offered a silent prayer and a hand of comfort, knowing that the pain she felt echoed in the hearts of many others.

The next morning, the sun rose on a town still reeling from the previous night's events. The air smelled of smoke and blood, but a new determination shimmered beneath the surface. The people of Dust Devil Gulch, battered but unbroken,

Justice Prevails

began the long, arduous process of rebuilding their lives. The scars would remain, physical reminders of the battle, and the emotional wounds would take longer to heal. However, there was a different sort of quietude in the valley now—a quietude born of courage, resilience, and a shared sense of purpose.

Elias, joined by Martha, Fitzwilliam and Sarah, made plans for the reconstruction of the town, ensuring that those wounded received the necessary medical attention. They organized relief efforts for the families who had lost their homes, and worked tirelessly to restore a sense of normalcy.

Their victory in the gunfight was merely the first step. The true fight was in rebuilding their community, ensuring that justice prevailed not only in legal terms but also in their lives.

Sarah, ever practical, began to compile a detailed report of the events, ensuring that the crimes committed by Thorne and his associates would not be forgotten. She also sought to unveil the network that had supported Thorne's operations, hoping to prevent future acts of violence and corruption. Though tedious and demanding, her work was crucial in ensuring that the victory at Dust Devil Gulch would not be in vain. It would become a testament to the importance of justice, reminding all that even amidst despair and violence, the truth would prevail.

Man From Tennessee

Weeks turned into months. Dust Devil Gulch slowly began to heal. New buildings rose from the ashes of the old, and the town square, though still scarred, regained its vibrancy.

The memory of the battle remained, a stark reminder of the price of freedom, but it also served as a symbol of the indomitable spirit of the people who had refused to surrender. Their resilience, born from the ashes of conflict, became a legend whispered from campfire to campfire, a story that inspired others to stand up against injustice and oppression. Justice, it turned out, wasn't a single moment of triumph; it was a long, arduous journey of rebuilding, healing, and the enduring hope for a better future. The story of Dust Devil Gulch became a testament to the enduring strength of the human spirit in its quest for justice, a story that would be told and retold for generations to come.

Chapter 24

Unexpected Losses

The quietude of the following days was a deceptive calm.

The dust had settled, literally and figuratively, on Dust Devil Gulch. The celebratory atmosphere, fleeting as it was, had evaporated, leaving behind a residue of sorrow and loss that hung heavier than the lingering smell of gunpowder. The celebratory gunfire had faded, replaced by the quiet sobs of widows and the hushed whispers of orphans. The jubilation of victory felt hollow, a discordant note in the symphony of grief that now filled the town.

Elias, though physically weary, found himself unable to rest. The weight of responsibility, the knowledge that he had overseen a victory purchased at a devastating cost, pressed down on him. He had fought for justice and won, yet the triumph felt incomplete, tinged with an unbearable sadness. He wandered through the town, a ghost in the pale light of the early morning sun, his gaze drawn to the makeshift graves dug hastily in the outskirts of the town.

Man From Tennessee

Each newly turned mound of earth represented a life lost,
a family shattered… a future stolen.

He stopped before a small, crudely made cross fashioned
from two pieces of driftwood. Carved into the wood were the
initials "J.H." He remembered John Hamill, a quiet, unassuming
man who had always seemed to be in the right place at the
right time, a steadfast ally in the fight against Thorne. He had
been a rock of stability, his calm demeanor a stark contrast to
the volatile situation. Now, he lay beneath the unforgiving
earth. Elias ran a hand over the rough wood of the cross, a
silent acknowledgment of his loss. The grief was a physical
weight, a heavy cloak wrapping around his heart.

The town's blacksmith, a grizzled veteran named Silas,
approached Elias, his eyes red-rimmed and swollen. Silas, a
man of few words, offered Elias a gruff nod, his hand resting on
his own shoulder. He didn't need to speak. The shared sorrow
hung heavy between them, a silent understanding forged in the
crucible of shared loss. Silas had lost his nephew in the battle, a
young man barely out of his teens.

The boy, full of life and ambition, had dreamt of becoming
a renowned rancher, his eyes bright with the vision of his own
vast holdings. Those dreams lay buried with him, consumed by
the violence that had swept through Dust Devil Gulch.

Unexpected Losses

That evening, a somber gathering was held at Old Man Fitzwilliam's ranch. The air was thick with grief, the silence punctuated by the occasional heartbroken sob. The townsfolk had gathered not to celebrate victory but to mourn their fallen. A simple wooden table held a collection of photographs and personal mementos—a worn leather-bound book, a child's drawing, a woman's embroidered handkerchief. Each item was a poignant reminder of the lives lost, the vibrant tapestry of Dust Devil Gulch irrevocably torn.

Martha Jenkins, her face streaked with tears, placed a single, wilting red rose on the table, a symbol of remembrance for her own brother, who had perished alongside John Hamill.

Her voice, normally so strong and resolute, was now barely a whisper as she spoke of his courage, unwavering loyalty, and the light he had brought to their lives. Her grief was palpable, raw, a testament to the deep bonds that had been severed by the violence.

Old Man Fitzwilliam offered a short, heartfelt eulogy, his usual mischievous twinkle replaced by a profound sadness. He spoke of the courage of the fallen, of their unwavering commitment to justice, of the legacy they had left behind. Though choked with emotion, his voice carried the weight of the town's shared sorrow, a collective lament for the lives lost.

Man From Tennessee

He spoke of the shared commitment to rebuild the town, both physically and emotionally and spiritually. He spoke of the need for a healing process, as much for the community as for the individuals bearing the wounds of the conflict. He highlighted the resilience of the human spirit, even in the face of unbearable loss. Though imbued with sorrow, his words offered a glimmer of hope, a promise of a future where their sacrifice would not be in vain.

Ever the pragmatist, Sarah had begun to systematically document the losses, creating a meticulous record of each life taken. Her efforts were not merely a matter of bureaucratic necessity but a profound act of remembrance, a way of honoring the fallen and ensuring that their sacrifices would be recognized. She had compiled a list of the casualties, detailing not only their names but also their contributions to the town and the fight against Thorne. Despite its tragic nature, her list was a testament to their collective spirit, a reminder of the lives woven into the fabric of Dust Devil Gulch. Each name on her list, each carefully recorded detail, served as a monument to a life lived, a life cut short. Her efforts' careful detail and systematic nature reflected the depth of her sorrow and her resolve to keep the memories of the fallen alive.

Unexpected Losses

Elias, listening to the stories and testimonials, felt a renewed sense of determination. The grief, though immense, would not consume him. He would channel his sorrow into action, into a renewed commitment to building a better future for Dust Devil Gulch, a future worthy of the sacrifices that had been made. The battle wounds were deep, both physical and emotional, but the town possessed a strength and resilience that would see them through this ordeal. Their unity, forged in the crucible of conflict, was stronger than ever. The fallen would be mourned, their stories would be told, and their memory would fuel the town's drive to rebuild their shattered community. Their victory was a testament to their bravery and the depth of their collective spirit, a legacy that would inspire generations to come.

The next few weeks were a blur of activity, the town slowly emerging from the shadow of the recent battle. The rebuilding process was long and arduous, each step forward a testament to the community's indomitable spirit. The work was physically and emotionally demanding, but the townspeople worked tirelessly, driven by a shared purpose and the memory of those they had lost. The reconstruction was more than just repairing buildings; it was a collective act of healing, a testament to the enduring strength of the human spirit in the face of tragedy.

Elias, along with Martha, Fitzwilliam and Sarah, took on the role of leaders, guiding and coordinating the efforts of the town. They sought to create a community that honored the memory of those lost, a town that would stand as a symbol of resilience and hope in the face of adversity. The rebuilding of Dust Devil Gulch was a tangible expression of their shared grief and their unwavering determination to create a future free from the oppression and injustice they had so recently overcome. The reconstruction went beyond bricks and mortar; it involved rebuilding lives, shattered spirits, and a future that must not forget the cost of freedom. Dust Devil Gulch would rise from the ashes, a testament to the enduring power of the human spirit, a legacy of courage, loss, and the unwavering pursuit of justice.

Chapter 25
A Moment of Reflection

The sun dipped below the horizon, painting the Wyoming sky in fiery hues of orange and crimson. Elias sat atop a windswept ridge, the vast expanse of prairie stretching before him like a rumpled velvet cloth. Below, Dust Devil Gulch nestled in the valley, a patchwork of newly repaired buildings and the scars of recent battle still visible. The air, cleansed by the recent rains, carried the scent of sagebrush and pine, a fragrance both comforting and melancholic. He had sought this solitude, this vantage point from which to survey not just the physical landscape, but the landscape of his own soul.

The past few weeks had been a whirlwind of activity, a frantic dance between grief and rebuilding. He had helped carry the fallen to their resting places, listened to the whispered grief of widows, and witnessed the stoic resilience of the townsfolk. He had watched Martha Jenkins, her face etched with sorrow, tend to her brother's small, unadorned grave, a testament to the depth of her loss and her unwavering strength. He had seen Sarah meticulously document the casualties, her work a quiet act of remembrance, a way of ensuring that the sacrifices of those lost were not forgotten. Old Man Fitzwilliam's eyes filled with a sadness that belied his usual mischievous twinkle had led the town's mourning, providing a solace that transcended the spoken word.

Elias had played his part, coordinating the rebuilding efforts and ensuring that justice was served, not just in the punishment of Thorne and his gang but also in the creation of a fairer, more equitable Dust Devil Gulch. But amidst the chaos and activity, he had found little time for introspection, for the quiet contemplation necessary to process the magnitude of what he had witnessed. Now, perched on this lonely ridge, he allowed himself to reflect as the last vestiges of daylight faded.

His journey had been long and arduous, a relentless pursuit of justice that had taken him from the dusty plains of his childhood to the tumultuous streets of Denver and finally to this small, hard-scrabble town in Wyoming. He had witnessed brutality, faced down outlaws, and experienced loss, both personal and communal. He had seen the best and worst of humanity, their capacity for both incredible kindness and unspeakable cruelty.

He thought of his father, a man who had instilled in him a strong sense of right and wrong, a belief in the power of justice, even in the face of overwhelming odds. He remembered the lessons his father had taught him, which had guided him through the darkest times. The memory of his father's steady hand on his shoulder and his quiet words of encouragement offered a comforting presence in this moment of introspection.

He recalled his early days in Dust Devil Gulch, the initial skepticism and mistrust that had greeted his arrival. He had been an outsider, an unwelcome intrusion into their established order. Yet, through perseverance and a demonstrable commitment to their cause, he earned their respect, trust, and loyalty. He had become part of their community, woven into the fabric of their lives.

The confrontation with Thorne had been brutal, a violent culmination of years of oppression and injustice. He had watched men and women, friends and neighbors, fall beneath the onslaught of gunfire. He had felt the raw, visceral fear that grips you in the face of death and the cold certainty that he might not survive. But he had also witnessed moments of incredible courage, selfless acts of bravery that had saved lives and turned the tide of the battle. He had learned that true strength wasn't measured solely in physical prowess but in the unwavering resolve to fight for what's right, even when the odds were stacked against you.

Man From Tennessee

Elias traced the outline of a distant mountain range with his finger. The image mirrored the contours of his own inner landscape, a terrain that had been shaped and reshaped by the past few months' events. The victory over Thorne was bittersweet. Dust Devil Gulch was safe, but the price had been steep. He had lived through the ordeal, but a part of him remained on that dusty battlefield, buried beneath the earth alongside those he had fought beside.

He thought of the scars that marred his body, physical reminders of the battle that had scarred him profoundly. He had lost friends, comrades, people who had fought shoulder to shoulder with him and who had shared his dreams of a better future. Their faces flickered in his mind's eye: John Hamill, the quiet blacksmith whose steadiness had been a source of comfort; Martha's brother, whose youthful idealism had been extinguished too soon; and the countless others whose names he would never forget.

These were the ghosts he carried within, the quiet echoes of loss that would forever accompany him. He understood now that there was no true escaping consequences, that even in victory, there was a price to be paid. But it was a price he was willing to bear, for he had fought for justice, and he had found

A Moment of Reflection

it, albeit amidst the ruins of his past and the heavy weight of sorrow.

The moon, a silver disc in the deepening twilight, cast long shadows across the land. A sense of peace settled over him as the stars began to emerge, painting the night sky with their celestial brilliance. He had found a kind of acceptance, not a resignation to fate but an understanding of the complex tapestry of life and its unpredictable twists and turns. The burden of responsibility still weighed heavily on his shoulders, but it no longer crushed him. He had come to terms with the consequences of his actions and found strength in his own resilience.

He stood up, silhouetted against the backdrop of the moonlit landscape. Dust Devil Gulch lay below, bathed in the soft glow of the moon. He would return to the town, to the work that still needed to be done, to the lives that needed mending.

He would continue to fight for a better future, for a world where justice would prevail, even if it was a future haunted by the ghosts of the past. He understood that he would never forget those lost, but that their memories would be a constant reminder of the importance of his efforts, a beacon guiding him on his path.

Man From Tennessee

The wind whispered through the tall grass, carrying with it the echoes of laughter and the soft murmur of prayers. He breathed in the cool night air, feeling a sense of profound serenity, a deep quietude that had eluded him for so long. He had endured, he had fought, he had won. And in the quiet stillness of the Wyoming night, he had finally found peace.

He knew the journey wasn't over; there would be more battles to face and more challenges to overcome. But he would face them armed not only with his strength but with the wisdom gained from his experiences and the unwavering resolve that his past had forged. The quietude of the night was his reward and the promise of a dawn that would break over a rebuilt Dust Devil Gulch—a future worthy of the sacrifices made. The setting sun had brought an end to one chapter, but the story was far from over. His story was just beginning.

Chapter 26
Life after the Storm

The moon hung heavy in the inky sky, casting long, skeletal shadows across the valley as Elias rode back toward Dust Devil Gulch. The silence of the night was broken only by the rhythmic thud of his horse's hooves and the occasional mournful cry of a coyote. He'd spent the last few hours alone, wrestling with the ghosts of the past, allowing himself the quiet reflection he so desperately needed. The peace he'd found atop that ridge, however fragile, was a balm to his weary soul. He knew the scars remained, both physical and emotional, but they no longer felt like gaping wounds but rather etched lines on a map, charting a journey he'd survived.

Dust Devil Gulch, bathed in the silvery moonlight, looked different now. The devastation was still evident, but there was a new energy, a palpable sense of purpose in the air. The broken buildings were slowly being mended; the streets were cleared of debris, a testament to the community's fierce determination to rise from the ashes.

Man From Tennessee

He found Sarah at her cabin, a small, sturdy structure
nestled at the edge of town. The repairs were nearly complete;
fresh paint shone brightly against the weathered wood, and the
smoke curling from the chimney suggested a warm fire within.
The cabin itself symbolized the town's rebirth, a beacon of
hope in the wake of devastation. The wildflowers Sarah had
planted around the perimeter were already blooming, a
vibrant splash of color against the muted tones of the
surrounding landscape.

"Elias," she said, her voice soft, her eyes reflecting the
firelight. She stood in the doorway, a steaming mug in her
hands, her face etched with a mixture of tiredness and
contentment. The events of the past weeks had aged her, but
there was a strength in her bearing that belied her weariness.
The dark circles under her eyes spoke of sleepless nights spent
poring over records, ensuring that every fallen soldier was
remembered and properly documented, their names etched in
the town's heart and the official records.

He dismounted, handing his reins to a passing stable hand.
"How are you, Sarah?" he asked, his voice raspy from the dust
and the long ride.

Life after the Storm

"Tired, but grateful," she replied, offering him a mug. "The cabin's almost finished. It feels right... to be here, to be rebuilding."

He took the mug, the warmth spreading through his chilled hands. "It's more than just a cabin, Sarah. It's a symbol of everything we've fought for, a testament to our resilience."

They sat by the fire, a comfortable silence settling between them. They had an unspoken understanding, a bond forged in the crucible of shared trauma. They had both witnessed the brutal reality of the confrontation with Thorne, seen friends and neighbors fall, and felt the chilling breath of death. But they had survived, their spirits unbroken. They had become fiercely loyal to one another, two individuals who found solace in each other's resilience.

Over the next few weeks, Elias dedicated himself to the rebuilding effort, working alongside Sarah and the townsfolk. The process wasn't easy, fraught with setbacks and disagreements, but the sense of shared purpose bound them together. They organized the construction of new buildings, secured supplies, and coordinated the efforts of the volunteers. Elias, respected for his leadership and unwavering commitment, quickly became a central figure in the revitalization project.

Man From Tennessee

He found himself increasingly drawn to Sarah. Her intelligence, quiet strength, and unwavering dedication to justice resonated deeply within him. Their shared experiences had created an unbreakable bond, a connection that went beyond friendship. He saw in her eyes the same weariness, the same ghosts of the past, but also a flickering flame of hope for the future. He understood that she needed time, time to heal, to come to terms with the trauma she had endured. He would give her that time, patience and understanding, allowing their relationship to blossom organically.

One evening, they sat on the porch of Sarah's cabin, watching the sun dip below the horizon, painting the sky in shades of gold and crimson. The air was taken by the aroma of pine and sagebrush, a fragrance of both sorrow and resilience.

"It feels strange," Sarah said, her voice barely a whisper. "To see the sunset and to feel...peaceful. To know that we've survived."

Elias nodded, placing a comforting hand on hers. "We did. We survived, Sarah. And we'll rebuild. We'll make this town stronger, even better than before."

The quiet strength in her grip was a reassuring weight in his hand. He knew that the rebuilding of Dust Devil Gulch

Life after the Storm

wasn't just about brick and mortar; it was about rebuilding
lives, mending broken spirits, and forging a new community
built on the foundation of shared resilience and unwavering
hope.

The integration into the community was gradual but
profound. Elias, initially viewed as an outsider, had earned
their respect and trust through his actions and his unwavering
commitment to their cause. He learned their customs, listened
to their stories, and shared in their struggles and triumphs. The
town's elders, initially cautious, began to seek his counsel,
valuing his wisdom and experience. The children, initially
wary, began to see him not as a stranger but as a protector, a
figure who represented hope and stability in their shattered
world.

Old Man Fitzwilliam's eyes still tinged with sadness, but
his twinkle was restored, and he became a close friend and
mentor. He shared tales of the town's history, stories of
resilience and triumph over adversity. Fitzwilliam, a living
repository of the town's collective memory, helped Elias
understand the unique character of Dust Devil Gulch, its
strength and spirit. His wisdom, dispensed with gentle humor,
eased the transition, helping Elias find his place within the
community.

Man From Tennessee

He also found camaraderie amongst the other survivors, forming deep friendships with men and women who had fought alongside him. The shared experience had forged unbreakable bonds, creating a support system that helped them navigate the emotional aftermath of the battle. The quiet strength of these connections was a constant reminder of the human capacity for resilience, the power of community, and the enduring nature of hope.

Evenings were often spent around the fire at Sarah's cabin, sharing stories, laughter, and quiet moments of reflection. The memories of the battle were never far away, but they were no longer the dominant narrative. They were interspersed with tales of dreams for the future and plans for a town rebuilt physically, emotionally, and spiritually.

The arrival of spring brought with it a renewed sense of optimism. The landscape, once scarred and desolate, was bursting with new life. Wildflowers carpeted the meadows, birdsong filled the air, and the scent of pine and sagebrush was invigorating and hopeful. It was a fitting backdrop to the town's transformation. The spirit of Dust Devil Gulch, bruised but not broken, was rising again, stronger and more unified than ever. Elias and Sarah, in their quiet way, were at the heart of this renaissance; their love for each other and their dedication to the town was a testament to the power of the human spirit to overcome adversity and build a brighter future from the ruins of the past. The rebuilding was far from over, but in the gentle spring breeze and the blossoming of new life, Elias felt the promise of a future worth fighting for, a future where justice and peace would prevail. The ghosts of the past would remain, but they would not define their future. They would be a reminder, a testament to the strength forged in the crucible of loss, a strength that would continue to shape and guide them in their journey toward a new beginning. The sun, rising each day over the reborn Dust Devil Gulch, was a promise of a brighter tomorrow.

Chapter 27

A New Normal

The rebuilding of Dust Devil Gulch wasn't merely a physical undertaking; it was a spiritual rebirth, a slow, painstaking process of mending broken buildings and hearts. Elias found himself deeply immersed in this collective healing, his own wounds slowly knitting together as he worked alongside the townsfolk. He learned the rhythm of their lives, the subtle nuances of their interactions, the unspoken language of shared experience. He discovered a camaraderie among the survivors, a bond forged in the crucible of shared trauma that transcended the superficial boundaries of friendship. These were people who had seen the worst of humanity yet retained an unshakeable faith in its inherent goodness. It was an inspiring testament to the resilience of the human spirit.

His days were filled with the practicalities of rebuilding— hauling lumber, mixing mortar, coordinating volunteers, and mediating disputes. Yet, these physical tasks were interwoven with the emotional tapestry of the community's recovery. He listened to their stories, recounting loss and grief, and the quiet moments of shared memory, each tale adding another layer to his understanding of Dust Devil Gulch. He became familiar with the faces of the fallen, learning their names, their stories, their lives, ensuring that their sacrifices were not forgotten. It was a sacred duty, a solemn commitment that bound him inextricably to the town.

Ever the steadfast anchor, Sarah remained a constant source of strength and inspiration. Their relationship deepened organically, nourished by shared experiences and mutual commitment to the town's resurgence. There were no grand declarations of love or sweeping romantic gestures; their bond was forged in the fires of adversity, a quiet understanding transcending words. They worked side-by-side, sharing burdens, celebrating small victories, and finding solace in each other's presence. Evenings spent by the fire, recounting the day's events were filled with a quiet contentment that belied the enormity of their collective undertaking.

The town, too, was transforming. The scarred landscape was slowly yielding to the relentless optimism of its inhabitants. New buildings rose from the rubble, each a testament to the community's unwavering spirit. Children's laughter echoed through the streets, a joyous counterpoint to the somber memories of the past. The rhythmic clang of the blacksmith's hammer, the cheerful chatter of the women mending clothes, and the low hum of conversation in the general store were the sounds of a town rediscovering its lifeblood.

Elias found himself increasingly drawn to the simpler aspects of life in Wyoming. The vast expanse of the prairie, the breathtaking sunsets, and the crisp mountain air filled him with a profound sense of peace he had never known before. He learned to appreciate the subtle beauty of the natural world, finding solace in the rhythm of the seasons, the cyclical nature of life and death, and the promise of renewal. The harsh realities of survival had stripped away the superficialities, leaving him with a deeper understanding of himself, his values, and his place in the world.

He began to ride again, not as a lone gunslinger seeking vengeance, but as a man at peace with himself, a man who found solace in the solitude of the vast Wyoming landscape. He would spend hours on horseback, traversing the rolling hills, allowing the wind to clear his mind, the silence to quiet his soul. These solitary journeys were not escapes but rather opportunities for reflection, for introspection, and for connecting with the land and with himself. He found a new kind of strength, a strength born not of violence but of resilience, a strength rooted in the quiet dignity of simple living.

His relationship with Old Man Fitzwilliam deepened, and the old man became a mentor and a friend. Fitzwilliam shared stories of the town's history, stories of hardship and resilience that resonated deeply with Elias's experiences. He learned of the town's pioneers, struggles and triumphs, and unwavering determination to build a life in this unforgiving land. It was a history that spoke of perseverance, the power of community, and the human spirit's ability to overcome adversity. The old man's wisdom, shared with a gentle smile and a twinkle in his eye, helped Elias find his footing in this new life.

Elias's acceptance into the community was not a sudden event but a gradual process, a quiet unfolding of trust and respect. He earned his place not through force or intimidation but through his unwavering commitment to the town's revival. His actions spoke louder than words, his selfless dedication to the rebuilding effort demonstrating his sincere commitment to their shared future. He became a trusted advisor, a friend, a leader, a symbol of hope in a town struggling to overcome its past. His influence extended beyond the practical aspects of rebuilding; he fostered a spirit of unity, reminding the town's folk of their shared strength and their collective ability to overcome even the most daunting challenges. He became an integral part of the fabric of Dust Devil Gulch.

One evening, as the sun dipped below the horizon, painting the sky in vibrant hues of orange and purple, Elias and Sarah sat on the porch of her cabin. The air was filled with pine and sagebrush, a fragrance of resilience and renewal. They had come so far and survived so much, and yet, the journey was far from over. But now, as they looked toward the future, it was with a sense of hope, of anticipation, of the promise of a brighter tomorrow.

"It's... peaceful," Sarah murmured, her voice soft, her gaze fixed on the distant horizon. "Dust Devil Gulch is coming back to life."

Elias nodded, his hand resting gently on hers. "Yes," he said, his voice filled with quiet satisfaction. "We've built it back stronger than before. We've learned to rebuild not just our homes and but our lives."

Their silence was filled with unspoken words, a shared understanding of all they had endured, and the hope that permeated their shared future. The past remained a constant reminder of the sacrifices made, but it was no longer a shadow that threatened to consume them. It was a foundation upon which they built a stronger, more unified community.

The new normal wasn't an erasure of the past but an acceptance of it, a turning toward a future built on resilience, hope, and a profound sense of community. Dust Devil Gulch was reborn, and Elias found his place not just within its borders, but within its heart. The long road to recovery stretched ahead, but they would face it together, their spirits unbroken, their hope undiminished. The rising sun over the reborn town was a promise of a future worthy of their sacrifices, a future where justice prevailed, and the scars of the past served as reminders of their enduring strength.

Chapter 28
Looking Toward the Future

The crisp morning air bit at Elias's cheeks, a familiar sting that no longer held the chill of despair. He stood at the edge of town, gazing at the sprawling Wyoming landscape, the vastness mirroring the boundless possibilities that stretched before him. Dust Devil Gulch, once a ghost town etched with the scars of violence and loss, is now pulsed with renewed energy and a vibrant testament to the resilience of its people. The rebuilding wasn't just about bricks and mortar; it was about rebuilding lives, mending broken spirits, and forging a future built on hope and shared purpose.

He watched children chase tumbleweeds across the newly paved streets, their laughter echoing through the rebuilt buildings, a joyous soundtrack to the town's resurgence. The rhythmic clang of the blacksmith's hammer; the scent of baking bread wafting from the general store were the sounds of a community finding its footing, reclaiming its identity, and embracing a new dawn. He thought of Sarah, her quiet strength a constant source of inspiration. Their relationship, born amidst the ashes of destruction, had blossomed into something profound, a silent understanding that transcended words. They had shared the burden of grief and the weight of responsibility; now, they shared the joy of rebuilding, the quiet contentment of a future slowly unfolding.

Elias's own transformation was as remarkable as the town's. The hardened gunslinger, haunted by a past filled with violence, had found a different kind of strength, a strength born not of vengeance but of resilience. Once a means of escape, the solitary rides across the prairie had become moments of profound reflection. The vastness of the land, The plains' silence provided a sanctuary for his soul, allowing him to confront his demons, reconcile with his past, and embrace a future defined by peace and purpose.

He had learned the land's rhythm and the seasons' subtle nuances. He understood the delicate balance of nature, the cyclical nature of life and death, and the enduring power of renewal. The harsh realities of survival had stripped away the superficial, revealing a deeper appreciation for the simple joys of life—the warmth of a crackling fire, the companionship of friends, the comforting presence of Sarah. He had discovered a sense of belonging, a connection to a community that had embraced him, not as an outsider, but as one of their own.

Looking Toward the Future

His relationship with Old Man Fitzwilliam had deepened, and the old man's wisdom provided a compass for navigating future challenges. Fitzwilliam, a repository of Dust Devil Gulch's history, had shared tales of hardship and perseverance, stories that echoed Elias's own experiences, strengthening his resolve and reminding him that even in the darkest of times, the human spirit could endure and triumph. The old man's unwavering faith in the town's potential had been infectious, a constant source of inspiration during the arduous rebuilding process.

But the future wasn't without its challenges. The economic recovery would be slow, the scars of the past would linger, and new challenges would inevitably arise. There were still whispers of discontent, murmurs of doubt, lingering shadows of fear. Some still mourned the losses, their grief a constant companion. The rebuilding, both physical and emotional, was far from complete. There were still cracks in the foundations, both literal and metaphorical, that needed to be addressed.

Elias knew that the true test of Dust Devil Gulch's resilience lay not in overcoming the immediate aftermath of the disaster but in navigating the long, arduous path toward a sustainable future. He understood that the town's survival depended on physical reconstruction and the ongoing cultivation of unity, cooperation, and hope. He knew that he, along with Sarah and the rest of the community, had a critical role in ensuring that the town survived and thrived.

The task ahead was daunting but not insurmountable. Elias had witnessed firsthand the strength and resilience of the Dust Devil Gulch community. He had seen them overcome the unimaginable, their spirits unbroken despite overwhelming odds. He had faith in their ability to face the challenges ahead, to build a future worthy of their sacrifices, a future where justice prevailed, and the scars of the past served as reminders of their enduring strength.

He had learned the importance of community, the power of collective action, and the transformative power of shared purpose. He had found a sense of belonging, a connection to something larger than himself. He had also learned the value of forgiveness for himself and others. He had come to terms with his own past, accepting the shadows while embracing the light.

His nights were now filled not with the haunting echoes of gunfire but with the gentle sounds of Sarah's breathing beside him, the quiet rhythm of their shared life. He spent his days working alongside the townsfolk, his hands calloused but his spirit renewed. He had found purpose in helping others, rebuilding homes and lives. He had become an integral part of

Looking Toward the Future

Dust Devil Gulch, not through power or dominance, but through service and compassion.

The future held uncertainties, but it also held the promise of a brighter tomorrow. Elias faced it with quiet confidence, a newfound sense of peace, and a deep understanding of his strength. He knew the road ahead would be long and challenging, but he also knew he was not alone. He had Sarah, his friends in Dust Devil Gulch, and the enduring spirit of the West to guide him. The rising sun over the reborn town promised a future worthy of their sacrifices, a future where the ghosts of the past were finally laid to rest and hope bloomed anew. The rebuilding of Dust Devil Gulch was a testament to the human spirit's unwavering capacity for resilience, a symbol of the possibility of new beginnings, even in the face of unimaginable tragedy. As Elias looked toward the horizon, he saw not a desolate landscape scarred by violence but a vibrant tapestry woven with threads of hope, resilience, and unwavering faith in the power of community. He saw a future worth fighting for, a future worth building, filled with the promise of peace and prosperity for Dust Devil Gulch and himself. The journey had been arduous, but the destination, finally, was within sight.

Chapter 29

The Legacy of the West

The wind, a constant companion across the Wyoming plains, whispered secrets through the tall grass, carrying with it the scent of sagebrush and the faint echo of distant thunder. Elias sat on the porch of the newly rebuilt saloon, a mug of lukewarm coffee warming his hands. The setting sun painted the sky in fiery orange and deep purple hues, casting long shadows across the revitalized Dust Devil Gulch. He watched as Sarah emerged from the general store, her silhouette framed against the warm glow of the evening light. Her presence, a quiet anchor in his life, filled him with a contentment he hadn't known existed before the devastation.

The transformation of Dust Devil Gulch had been a testament to the enduring spirit of the West, a spirit forged in the crucible of hardship and tempered by unwavering resilience. It wasn't merely the physical rebuilding that mattered; it was the rebirth of a community, the forging of new bonds, the rediscovery of shared purpose. Elias had witnessed firsthand the human spirit's incredible capacity to endure, overcome, and rebuild even amidst the ashes of tragedy. He thought of the long, arduous days of clearing rubble, of hauling timber, of laying bricks. He recalled the moments of despair, the gnawing doubt, the heavy weight of responsibility. But through it all, the community had held together, bound by a shared determination to survive, to thrive.

The legacy of the West was etched into the very fabric of Dust Devil Gulch. It was a legacy of rugged individualism, unwavering determination, a fierce love for the land, and a deep respect for its challenges. It was a legacy of pioneers who had pushed the boundaries of civilization, faced adversity with grit and courage, and carved a life from the raw, untamed wilderness. This was the spirit that Elias had witnessed firsthand, the spirit that had fueled the town's remarkable resurgence.

He thought of Old Man Fitzwilliam, his eyes twinkling like distant stars, his voice a comforting rumble that carried tales of the old West. The old man had been a living archive of Dust Devil Gulch's history, his stories resonating with the timeless struggles and triumphs of the pioneers. Fitzwilliam's unwavering faith in the town, even during its darkest hours, had been a beacon of hope, inspiring Elias and others to persevere. His stories, steeped in the lore of the West, served as a powerful reminder of the indomitable spirit that had shaped this land and its people.

The vastness of the Wyoming landscape had always held a certain mystique, a power that both intimidated and inspired. It was a land of stark beauty, unforgiving terrain, and a relentless climate. It was a land that tested the limits of human endurance yet rewarded those who persevered with a profound sense of accomplishment and a deep connection to the earth. The expansive plains, the rugged mountains, the wild rivers were all part of the fabric of the West, shaping the character of its inhabitants and forging a unique cultural identity.

Elias's own journey mirrored the spirit of the West. He had arrived in Dust Devil Gulch, a hardened gunslinger haunted by his past, burdened by guilt. He'd found solace in the landscape's vastness, in the prairie's solitude. He'd confronted his demons, wrestled with his inner turmoil, and ultimately emerged transformed, his spirit tempered by the harsh realities of survival. He had come to understand the importance of community, the power of collective action, and the transformative impact of shared purpose. The rebuilding of Dust Devil Gulch had been more than just a physical undertaking; it was a spiritual journey, a testament to the power of redemption.

The economic recovery would be a long, slow process. There were still challenges to overcome and obstacles to navigate. The scars of the past would linger, serving as reminders of the town's resilience. But Elias saw in the faces of his fellow townsfolk a renewed sense of hope, a determination to build a better future. Children's laughter echoed through the streets, a poignant counterpoint to the somber memories of the past. The scent of baking bread mingled with the scent of freshly cut timber, a fragrance of rebirth and renewed vitality.

He recalled the challenges they faced. The initial shock and grief following the disaster, the daunting task of clearing the debris, the scarcity of resources, the political maneuvering necessary to secure aid, and the constant fear of further attacks had all been overwhelming. Yet, they had persevered.

They had drawn strength from one another, their shared sense of community, and their unwavering belief in the future.

The spirit of the West was more than just a romantic notion; it was a way of life, a philosophy that embraced resilience, self-reliance, and a profound respect for the natural world. It was a legacy that had been passed down through

The Legacy of the West

generations, a heritage that continued to shape the lives of those who lived in its embrace. The people of Dust Devil Gulch were living embodiments of that legacy, embodying the spirit of pioneers who had faced adversity with unwavering courage and fortitude.

Elias knew that the true legacy of the West was not simply about conquering the land but about building a sustainable future, preserving its natural beauty, and fostering a community built on respect, cooperation, and mutual support. He saw Dust Devil Gulch not just as a town reborn but as a symbol of the enduring spirit of the West, a testament to the human capacity for resilience and a beacon of hope for the future.

The setting sun dipped below the horizon, casting a final, warm glow upon the town. As darkness fell, the stars emerged, twinkling like diamonds scattered across the velvet sky. Elias held Sarah's hand, their fingers intertwined, symbolizing their shared journey and future. The quiet contentment that settled over him was profound. He was no longer just a gunslinger, a man haunted by his past. He was a member of a community, a builder of a new future, a testament to the enduring spirit of the West. The journey had been long and arduous, but the destination, the promise of a brighter tomorrow, was finally within reach. The rebuilding of Dust Devil Gulch was more than just a physical accomplishment; it was a testament to the human spirit's indomitable capacity to overcome tragedy and forge a path toward a hopeful future, a future built on the resilient foundation of the enduring West. He knew, with a certainty that warmed him from the inside out, that the legacy of Dust Devil Gulch would live on, a symbol of hope and renewal for generations to come. The echoes of gunfire were finally silenced, replaced by the laughter of children and the quiet hum of a community finding its peace. And in that peace, Elias found his own.

Epilogue

A New Dawn

The dawn broke gently over the Wyoming plains, painting the eastern sky in soft hues of rose and gold. A gentle breeze rustled the leaves of the young aspen trees Elias had planted near their cabin, their delicate leaves shimmering like a thousand tiny mirrors reflecting the nascent light. The air, crisp and clean, carried the scent of pine and damp earth, a fragrance that spoke of renewal and promise. Sarah stirred beside him, her breath warm against his cheek. He watched her for a moment, the sunlight catching the strands of auburn hair escaping her braid, illuminating the gentle curve of her cheek and the peaceful serenity etched upon her features.

Their small cabin, built with his own hands, nestled snugly amongst the pines, a haven of peace amidst the vast, untamed wilderness.

Unlike the dust and debris-filled saloon of Dust Devil Gulch, this new home felt different. It wasn't merely a dwelling; it was a sanctuary, a testament to their shared journey, perseverance, and enduring love. The silence, punctuated only by the chirping of birds and the gentle whisper of the wind through the pines, was a welcome contrast to the echoes of gunfire and the cries of despair that had once haunted their days.

He rose carefully, not wanting to disturb her slumber, and stepped outside. The morning light bathed the landscape in a soft, golden glow, revealing the extent of their little plot of land. A small garden, bursting with vibrant wildflowers and herbs, bordered the cabin, a testament to Sarah's green thumb and her patient nurturing. Beyond the garden, a small herd of cattle grazed peacefully, a symbol of their burgeoning prosperity. He had learned so much from the old cowboys, their knowledge of the land and its rhythms, their patient ways, and things Elias had never dreamed of knowing or even needing to know. He had even started to appreciate the quiet solitude of the vast landscape, a place that had once felt like a prison but now felt like a sanctuary.

The rebuilding of Dust Devil Gulch had been a turning point, not just for the town but for him. It had been a crucible that had forged his spirit anew, tempering his rage and shaping his sense of purpose. He had gone from a hardened gunslinger, haunted by the ghosts of his past, to a man finding peace in the quiet rhythm of daily life, a man content with the simple

180

pleasures of honest labor and the love of a good woman. He remembered the days when he only knew violence and survival. It felt like a lifetime ago.

He ran his hand over the rough-hewn wood of the cabin's porch railing, the texture familiar and comforting. He thought of the long, arduous months, the sweat, the blisters, the constant ache in his back. He had poured his heart and soul into this place, a physical manifestation of his desire for a new beginning, a new life. And it wasn't just the physical work that had been transformative; it was the emotional labor of confronting his past, accepting his failings, and forging a path toward redemption.

The economic recovery of Dust Devil Gulch had been slow, a gradual healing of wounds both physical and emotional.

But it had happened. The town was slowly but surely returning to life, the scars of the past becoming faint reminders of their remarkable resilience. The laughter of children playing in the streets had replaced the sounds of fear and uncertainty. The scent of freshly baked bread and blooming flowers mingled with the smell of sawdust and horses, a heady mix that spoke of a community reborn. He had seen many people finding their way back to a life that could feel normal again.

He looked out across the vast expanse of the Wyoming plains, the morning mist clinging to the distant hills. He thought of Old Man Fitzwilliam, his stories still resonating in his mind, his wisdom echoing through the years. The old man had been right. The enduring spirit of the West was a powerful force capable of overcoming any obstacle and forging a path toward a brighter future. That spirit wasn't just about conquering the wilderness; it was about building communities, preserving the land, and fostering a sense of shared purpose.

Sarah emerged from the cabin, her hair neatly braided, her eyes shining with the joy of a new dawn. She wore a simple cotton dress, her beauty enhanced by the unadorned grace of her natural appearance. She carried a steaming mug of coffee, its rich aroma filling the morning air. As she approached him, he took her hand, their fingers intertwining, a silent testament to their love, their resilience, their shared dreams.

They stood together, silhouetted against the rising sun, their figures casting long shadows across the dew-kissed grass.

The silence between them was comfortable, a silent conversation filled with unspoken words, shared memories, and the quiet confidence of a future well-earned. He looked at her, truly looked at her, and felt an overwhelming sense of gratitude. Gratitude for her unwavering love, strength, faith in him, and unwavering belief in their shared future.

He knew their journey wasn't over. There would be new challenges, new obstacles, new storms and new weather. But they would face them together, hand in hand, their spirits tempered by the fires of adversity, their hearts strengthened by the bonds of love and community. Their life together was a testament to the West's enduring spirit, which valued resilience, perseverance, and the enduring strength of the human heart. The scars of their past would forever be a part of their story, but they would not define them. They would live on, not as ghosts of the past but as pioneers of a brighter future.

The sun climbed higher in the sky, casting its warm golden rays upon their little haven. The world was awakening around them, alive with the sounds and smells of a new day.

As they sipped their coffee, sharing a quiet moment of peace and contentment, Elias felt a profound sense of gratitude. He had found his redemption not in the smoke and echoes of gunfire but in the quiet joy of a new beginning, a new life, built upon the ashes of the past but strengthened by the enduring spirit of the West. The journey had been long and arduous, but they had arrived, and the future, once a distant and uncertain prospect, now stretched before them, bright and full of promise. This new dawn was not merely the beginning of a new day; it was the start of a new chapter in their lives, a chapter written not in violence and despair but in peace, love, and unwavering hope for a future filled with enduring strength. The West, they knew, was more than just a land; it was a spirit, an ethos, a legacy they were now privileged to carry forward. And they would carry it with pride, honor, and enduring faith in the enduring strength of the human heart. The quiet hum of the morning became the soundtrack of their new beginning.

Glossary

Chuck Wagon: A mobile kitchen used by cowboys and cattle drovers.

Branding: The process of marking cattle with a hot iron to identify ownership.

Dust Devil: A small, swirling whirlwind of dust and sand, common in arid regions.

Homestead Act: A series of United States federal laws that gave an applicant freehold title to government land.

Prairie Schooner: A covered wagon used by pioneers to transport their belongings during westward expansion.

Range War: A violent conflict over land and grazing rights between competing ranchers or settlers.